Published by Hashim Hakim, Copyright May 2013, Revised January 2019

ISBN: 9781983775529

AF581014

Book Cover Design: Hashim Hakim

Edited by: Sister Janiah X

Cover and back Photos: Justin "Jmilz" Milhouse- Detroit

FOREWORD

The Student Assistant Supreme Captain Grandmaster Anthony Muhammad

"My Brother, Hashim Hakim, is an example to the brothers of the N.O.I for his commitment towards propagating the faith. There are those who sell The Final Call Newspaper, and they are a blessing to our nation. But Brother Hashim not only sells the paper, he helps produce other men like himself. He is desirous of feeding our people knowledge, wisdom and understanding. So I say to everyone reading these words, this Brother Hashim Hakim-Muhammad, is priceless and should be studied. Brother Hashim is someone I have used to go throughout the Central Region where he has proven time and time again that his techniques are ABSOLUTELY SUCCESSFUL."

Brother Hashim poses with the Southwest Regional Captain Stephen Muhammad (far right).

The Most Honorable Elijah Muhammad, Messenger of Allah, speaks on The Muhammad Speaks Newspaper (The Final Call Newspaper) Sunday November 4, 1962.

There is truth in our paper, "Muhammad Speaks"! There are some of us who say we will give our lives for the truth or that we will die for Islam. Yet, we are not willing to go out amongst the public and offer the truth to our dead brother living right next door to us. Think over that!

The truth is right in our paper. Your dead brother living next door to you does not know it. Why won't you go knock on his door? Say, "Brother would you like to read this? Here it is." You are then helping to raise the dead. You are doing charitable work for the cause of truth. However, you say, "I cannot sell papers."

Why are you telling me, brother, that you will give your life? You cannot give your life for that which you will not give your time. Some of us show that when we sell the paper, we care nothing about the truth. ***We take the money we earn from selling the paper and use it for ourselves instead of using it for the truth, by paying for our papers.*** *You should be ashamed of yourselves.*

You should sell a million papers (in Detroit alone). The people are not rejecting the paper, they want it. ***It is you who are refusing to carry the paper to the people. You are the one****. Throughout the country, I find very little opposition to the Muhammad Speaks Newspaper. Everyone now wants to read what Muhammad is saying. I don't blame them. Anytime a man comes from under the chains and bondage of the White man, then speaks and says the things Muhammad is saying, I would walk 10 miles to buy one. If you give them to me to sell, I would not sleep until I was turned down by all the people with an arm full of papers left. Brothers, this paper will get you rest. It will bring life to you. It will* *unshackle you. It will establish you on something that is your own. Be ashamed of yourselves. You have the preaching. So go sell the paper of truth to the person who needs it.*

*Do your part of charity towards the truth. Don't say you don't have time to represent the truth, yet you have time to "**DIE FOR TRUTH**". Of which are you being honest?*

Allah is bringing light to a people that sit in darkness. All praises are due to Allah. There are many that have not even been in a meeting of Islam. The paper gets the truth to that population of people. The Christian world is in fire, but Islam will live in a cool place.

***NOTE TO THE MINISTER**: Our newspaper is very important. I am charging you with the responsibility of instilling in the followers at your Mosque, the spirit to put a successful effort into our own.*

"The paper must go in every home, every issue. The paper must not die because of lack of enthusiasm or effort.

***Note**: "What we are asking is small compared to what the devil is asking of us and even his own people. The devil will take people into his army for two and three years and some lose an arm, a leg or an eye or may even become paralyzed for his cause. Being asked to sell Muhammad speaks Newspaper is not as half as bad as that!"*

VOL. 1 NO. 1 MAY, 1979 50 CENTS

THE ULTIMATE CHALLENGE: THE SURVIVAL OF THE BLACK NATION

"WE MUST PUT OUR MINDS ON THE RAISING UP OF THE BLACK MAN IN AMERICA, IN THE CARIBBEAN, IN AFRICA AND WHEREVER BLACK PEOPLE ARE. WE MUST DEVELOP AND STRENGTHEN OUR CONNECTIONS AND BUILD BRIDGES OF UNDERSTANDING TO OUR PEOPLE ALL OVER THE WORLD."

— *Minister Louis Farrakhan*

"ISLAM IS TRUTH; ISLAM IS RIGHTEOUSNESS; ISLAM IS THE SUN OF LAW; ISLAM IS HELP TO THE HELPLESS POOR; ISLAM IS THE DIVINE LIGHT; ISLAM IS THE CRITERION OF JUDGEMENT; ISLAM IS FREEDOM, JUSTICE AND EQUALITY; ISLAM IS SUBMISSION TO THE WILL OF GOD."

— *The Honorable Elijah Muhammad*

THIS MONTH IN BRIEF . . .

(This message was delivered by the Honorable Minister Louis Farrakhan live via telephone conference to The Nation of Islam on Tuesday, April 26, 2011.)

"Let me personally thank the F.O.I. who go out from their homes with The Final Call Newspaper, to bring the Message of the Most Honorable Elijah Muhammad and his Minister to the people. The Final Call is a wonderful newspaper, filled with knowledge and wisdom. Every newspaper is really a small book. So when you take The Final Call, and study it, and then deliver it to our people, you are doing The Work of a minister. You should not fear to go out amongst our people to deliver The Message; for the Bible says in 1 Chronicles 16:22, "Touch not mine anointed, and do My Prophets no harm."

You are walking in the footsteps of the Prophets of God. And even though you may be evil spoken of, even though you may be rejected, even though sometimes we are attacked, yet, we are following in the Footsteps of the Prophets of GOD. There is no nobler task in this world than to imitate and emulate The Prophets of GOD. You are with The One Who ends all of the prophets, and ushers in The World of GOD Himself."

The Honorable Minister Louis Farrakhan

Excerpt from the Lecture **"WHAT IS A FATHER?"**
Delivered on June 18, 1995
Mosque Maryam Chicago, IL

"We have one of the finest newspapers of any group of Black people anywhere to be found on the earth. And I am deeply grateful and indebted to the F.O.I. for their dedicated service. They are not paper boys, but they are GREAT men.

They are not persons without aim and purpose, but they are little messengers of the Messenger bringing the divine message of Islam and the teachings of the Most Honorable Elijah Muhammad to our people.

And in that effort, they are providing an economic base that allows us independent education and to build schools and to buy farms and soon industry (factories) that will give employment opportunities to our people.

So every time you see one of these great young men or older men with that newspaper in their hand... get a newspaper in your hands."

A Man and His Mission
The Honorable Minister Louis Farrakhan

Once the man who is born for the mission meets "The Mission", it is love at first sight. And the marriage takes place. And the man and the mission become one.

So the only reason for the man's existence, the only thing that makes his life meaningful or with purpose, is that he at last has found what God has desired for him to do. So now everything that is around that person is measured by their commitment to that which he is born into the world to do.

Those who are truly sent can not escape what they are born in the world to do.

****

The Honorable Minister Louis Farrakhan (center)

"In every military, despite the occupation one may have, there is one thing every soldier must learn to do, and that is KNOW how to shoot a weapon.

It is the same with the F.O.I and the members of the Nation of Islam. Despite your title and post, every member in the Nation of Islam must know how to speak well, and represent The Final Call Newspaper."

Student Minister Donald Muhammad

St.Louis, Missouri

****

(From far left)Brother Shaquil and behind him Brother Malik, (center) Brother Akil and behind him, Brother Koran and Brother Hashim (Far Left)

Introduction

The intent of this manual is to make us thorough, complete and fully skilled in representing ourselves when it comes to sales, recruiting, obtaining customers, opening and closing sales with the proper handling of people, and the technique of timing. We will use The Final Call Newspaper as our demonstration tool, however just about any product and/or item will work. The name of this manual and course is The P.A.T.H. which stands for: **Patience, Attraction, Technique, Humility.**

In this manual you will learn:

What The Final Call newspaper is and what it consists of

What is "A CAUSE?"

How to find YOUR personal motivation for representing The Final Call Newspaper

The seeds of the P.A.T.H

How to handle Rejection

How to handle FEAR

How to consistently practice prayer and visualization techniques

How to carry out the action

Take care of your feet

Earn her Peace

What a typical day for me is like

Our Way of Devotion

Chapter 51 of the Holy Qur'an, Al-Dhåriyåt: The Scatterers, lays the basis for why we, who have signed the pledge card, the Form 4 and accepted the Universal Mission of the Most Honorable Elijah Muhammad, must adhere to our Sole Purpose.

Sole Purpose: To deliver the 17 million or more (Mentally) dead to the Lamb of God, the Most Honorable Elijah Muhammad.

sole

\ ˈsōl \

Definition of *Sole*
(Entry 1 of 4)

1a: being the only one (she was her mother's *sole* support)
b: having no sharer
2: functioning independently and without assistance or interference (let conscience be the *sole* judge)
3: belonging exclusively or otherwise limited to one usually specified individual, unit, or group

4: not married —used chiefly of women
5: *archaic* : having no companion : SOLITARY

I want you to take your time and carefully understand what you are about to read. This chapter from The Holy Qur'an in its entirety also lays the basis for why I have written this book. The introduction, the first 6 verses, and the commentary from Imam Maulana Muhammad, sets the tone for what we will be covering in this book. Let this mind be in you.

CHAPTER 51 Al-Dhåriyåt: The Scatterers (REVEALED AT MAKKAH: 3 sections; 60 verses)

Introduction Commentary to Chapter 51 by Maulana Muhammad Ali

The title of this chapter is taken from the mention of ***The Scatterers of Truth*** *in the first verse. Attention is drawn in the first section to the* ***gradual advancement of Truth****, which was daily gaining ground, and stress is laid upon the certainty of the judgment of the rejecters.*

The second section, opening with the announcement of the birth of a son to Abraham, which stands really for the ***birth of a new nation of righteous people****, deals with the fate of some previous nations who were judged because of their evil deeds.*

The third again, after an exhortation to seek refuge in Allåh, warns the opponents that their turn of good fortune is about to be ended and they shall be judged. It is an early Makkan revelation.

Commentary to be continued.......

SECTION 1 of Surah 51: Falsehood is doomed

In the name of Allåh, the Beneficent, the Merciful.

1 By those scattering broadcast!

2 And those bearing the load!

3 And those running easily!

4 And those distributing the Affair!—

5 What you are promised is surely true,

6 And the Judgment will surely come to pass.

Cont'd Commentary by Maulana Muhammad Ali:

6a. In the first four verses of this chapter, attention is called to certain facts by means of what is generally understood to be an **OATH**, for which see 37:1a, while the two verses that follow indicate the conclusion to which those facts lead. It is generally considered that by "those scattering broadcast" are meant the winds that raise up dust before the coming of a cloud; by the **"bearers of the load"** the clouds that carry rain; by the "easy runners" the winds that carry the clouds along, and by the "distributors" the winds that distribute the rain.

Attention is drawn in this description to a similar arrangement in the spiritual world by which Truth gradually advances. The seed of Truth is scattered broadcast in the first stage, while the bearing of the load or becoming **pregnant with Truth** is the second stage, the third being the strong desire to accept it, which makes one run for it without difficulty, while the fourth is its distribution to others. But we may as well say that attention is herein drawn to more manifest facts, to the scattering of Truth broadcast through the Holy Prophet and **his faithful followers**, which led to some bearing the load of it as if they had become pregnant with Truth, while others ran easily towards the acceptance of Truth. But they were not satisfied with mere acceptance; **they went to and fro to deliver to others the Truth and the Light, which they had received.**

In the existence of these groups of workers in the cause of Truth there was a clear sign that the triumph of **Islåm would soon be established in the land**.

7a. The description of heaven as full of paths is a scientific truth certainly unknown to the world 1,300 years ago. The paths in the heavens are the orbits of the various planets, and of the stars themselves; compared 36:40, where it is stated that "all float on in an orbit". 9a. Only those are turned away from the Truth who themselves turn away. 14a. For fitnah meaning persecution, see 2:191c. Tasting of persecution signifies receiving punishment for their persecution of the Muslims.

{My notes: In the above commentary by Maulana Muhammad Ali, the Oath could refer to our pledge and our Allegiances to The Master, His Messenger and His Divine Guidance amongst us in the Honorable Minister Louis Farrakhan.

The Scatterers, or distributors, refer to those of us who propagate the faith by distributing the affair. The affair is/are Islam and the Teachings of the Most Honorable Elijah Muhammad as taught to us by the Honorable Minister Louis Farrakhan and The Final Call Newspaper. Many will bear witness that our consistency in doing so has contributed to our gradual advancement and success in establishing mosques, ushering in the "New World", obtaining a wife or husband, economics, homes, friendships from all walks of life, Allah's protection, Forgiveness, Grace and Mercy.

The "Bearers of the Load" refer to those who are not only hearers of The Word, but "Doers" of The Word; the propagators of faith who are consistently cognizant of their "Sole Purpose."

"Cursed be the liars" could refer to those who hear but fail to obey, those of us who are neglectful of our duties, those who break their oaths, or those who committed publicly but secretly had not the intentions of fulfilling their obligations. The dutiful and the "Faithful Followers" are those of us who will be protected, forgiven and exalted. These will also be the MOST SUCCESSFUL in establishing Islam and ushering in the New World.}

1

What is The Final Call Newspaper?

In order for one to represent The Final Call Newspaper, one must first know the very essence of what it is. The Final Call Newspaper is a message dedicated to the Black man and woman in America and the world. The Final Call follows national and international news, health and coverage of political issues; as well as local urban media in various cities.

Firmly, The Final Call Newspaper delivers hard-hitting national and international headlines and perspectives. The Final Call aims to serve as an essential source of information for those who thirst for uncompromised reporting in today's arena of corporate driven media.

In order to sell The Final Call, it would be prudent to know the history behind it. The original version of The Final Call Newspaper was founded by the Most Honorable Elijah Muhammad in the 1930s as The Final Call to Islam. This small newspaper evolved into the Muhammad Speaks newspaper in the 1960s and attracted a circulation of 900,000 per week, with a monthly circulation of 2.5 million.

Today, the weekly Final Call Newspaper serves a readership of diverse economic and educational backgrounds and is distributed in North America, Canada, Europe, Africa, the Caribbean and spreading throughout the world.

The Final Call is a newspaper published in Chicago. It was founded in 1979 by the Honorable Minister Louis Farrakhan and serves as 'A message dedicated to the resurrection of the Black man and woman in

America and the world.' (See on the bottom left of the first page in every Final Call Newspaper.)

2

What is a "Cause"?

One definition of Cause is:

noun

1.

A person or thing that gives rise to an action, phenomenon, or condition.

Ex. The Most Honorable Elijah Muhammad gave rise and reform to the descendants of slaves here in the wilderness North America.

2.

A principle, aim, or movement that, because of a deep commitment, one is prepared to defend or advocate.

Ex. The Honorable Minister Louis Farrakhan devoted his life to the cause of the resurrection of the Black man woman in America and the world.

Chapter 17 in 1 Samuel tells the inspirational underdog story of David and Goliath. David's three older brothers had enlisted and were serving in the military. David's father sent him to take food and to see how his brothers were doing.

Upon arrival, David overheard the Philistine's best warrior, Goliath, openly mocking Israel and their God. Shocked to see Israel in fear and running from their open enemy, David was moved to anger.

Eliab, David's oldest brother, overheard David's inquiry and checks him. "Why have you come down here? You've only come to watch the battle!"

David responds: "Is there not a cause?"

What makes the students of The P.A.T.H. successful is that no matter how dark the hour is, no matter how many obstacles are in our path, no matter the weather, they never lose focus of their cause. They strive to keep their commitment and their duty Allah, themselves, their Nation and their communities.

Our Sole Purpose and our cause go hand in hand. Again, our Sole Purpose is to deliver our people to The Messenger of God to and to instill in them The Teachings of the Most Honorable Elijah Muhammad as taught to us by the Honorable Minister Louis Farrakhan.

The Honorable Minister Louis Farrakhan has taught us that the basis for community development is self improvement. If we improve self, we improve our community; for we are the community. In that order!

Remember point #4 of the Most Honorable Elijah Muhammad's Program is: Make your own neighborhood a decent place to live.

How do you do this? We have to constantly remain in our studies. Good starters are the **Study Guides (The Basis for Community Development)** that have been given to us by the Honorable Minister Louis Farrakhan, the Messenger's 12 Point Program in **Message to the Black Man** (Page 170), and **The Restrictive Law is Our Success.**

Once the person is introduced to "The Teachings", this process begins. Again, once we improve ourselves, we improve our communities. And this is how you reduce violence. This is how we make our communities a decent and safer place to live.

We have to remember that the solutions to the problems that we face as a people are within The Teachings of the Most Honorable Elijah Muhammad as taught to us by the Honorable Minister Louis Farrakhan. In that order!

When it comes to the condition of the darker people all over the earth, can you not see and bear witness that there is a need for our restoration physically, mentally, financially and spiritually? Can you not see the need for a leader, a Saviour and a champion who is unafraid to speak truth to power and show us how to contend with "Our Open-Enemies?"

Just as David witnessed his "So-called" leaders in fear of Goliath, the Honorable Minister Louis Farrakhan is and has witnessed Black leaders tremble with fear when it comes to speaking truth to power for the liberation of our people. We have a man like David in our midst today that is hurling truth at falsehood fearlessly. And just by distributing, delivering and spreading the truth in The Final Call Newspaper, we are aiding the Honorable Minister Louis Farrakhan in the cause of taking out our open enemy.

I want to make this very clear: I have been the top salesman at any and every sales job that I have ever held. Whether it was travel packages at AAA, the telecommunication department, or my music, I will not settle for second place. And there is one principle that ALWAYS gives me the edge...and that is "The Cause."

In other words, people are more susceptible to support a cause than a person; especially if that cause affects them personally. In sales, consumers want the best for their money. Don't you want the best of what you can afford to buy? A great salesman should be able to explain in straight words, “This is the best for what you are willing to spend.”

A great salesman asks questions. It is important to know what interests a person. And once you find out what interests a person, you can relate the best product you have to their interests and seal the deal most of the time. There are products that sell themselves because of the representation and/or quality of the product itself. These products just need a nice and attractive salesperson.

Then, there are products that are high quality and often times better than the highly marketed product. These products not only need a nice attractive distributor that knows The P.A.T.H., but they also need a person that can communicate that this product is of better quality than what you are used to supporting. Regardless of the cost, regardless of the sacrifice, the consumer will be compelled to consider the better option. This is the purpose and motivation for me writing and revising this manual.

The Final Call Newspaper has no legitimate competition when it comes to its purpose; (a message dedicated to the resurrection of the Black man and woman in America and the world).

“The Cause”, when it comes to why we distribute The Final Call Newspaper, is making our communities a decent and safer place to live. “The Cause” is to reduce violence in our community. “The Cause” is to show our people how to eat to live. “The Cause” is community development. We are taught by the Honorable Minister Louis Farrakhan that community development starts with self improvement. This is what the Final Call Newspaper consists of.

3

What is Your Motivation?

Now that you know what The Final Call is, it is important that you understand your role as a Final Call distributor. You must have a keen sense of what your Sole Purpose is. Understanding your purpose will fuel your motivation in whatever it is you set out to accomplish.

When it comes to the Final Call Newspaper, you are a Saviour. Let us look at the definition of the word savior.

Saviour: A person who rescues another from harm, danger or loss.

And if you study any Saviour or Messenger of Allah (God), there was always a degree of rejection from amongst their own people. This is common because initially, we don't like change or correction, especially coming from one amongst ourselves. Even more, we don't like to be taken out of our comfort zone.

It is important that you have the divine motive of resurrecting the people. The Honorable Minister Louis Farrakhan teaches us that motive is the will that determines the degree of power of the spirit to aid in what you do. In order for us to be extraordinary representatives of The Final Call Newspaper, we will need to understand why The Final Call Newspaper — the number one tool of resurrection — is so important. Our mission is to deliver the 17 million or more dead to the Lamb of God, the Most Honorable Elijah Muhammad. The Most Honorable Elijah Muhammad left us with the instructions to look, listen and follow the Minister's guidance.

Next to the Honorable Minister Louis Farrakhan himself, the unadulterated word that comes from Allah through the Messenger of

Allah and the Minister, contain the spirit that manifests change in all who receive that word. So the spirit that we encounter each and every time we see, hear and follow the word of God coming through the Minister, the person who reads The Final Call, encounters a similar experience when they read The Final Call Newspaper.

The more that person becomes exposed to the teachings of the Most Honorable Elijah Muhammad as taught to us by the Honorable Minister Louis Farrakhan, the better chance we have of accomplishing our Sole Purpose of resurrecting those who are mentally, spiritually, financially and morally dead.

Let us look into the meaning of dead. This definition comes directly from the Nation of Islam's Study Course on MESSAGE TO THE BLACK MAN.

Dead: no longer living or deathlike. It means lacking positive qualities, as of warmth, vitality, interest, brightness, brilliance, etc. It is characterized by little or no movement or activity; slack, stagnant, unresponsiveness and having the appearance of death. Also, as in electricity, it means having no current passing through (dead wire).

So if the mission is to deliver the mentally dead to the Messenger of God, and The Final Call Newspaper reaches people all over the world by the hundreds and thousands, it should now be apparent why The Final Call is the number one tool of the Nation of Islam when it comes to resurrecting our people. The Final Call has this kind of power.

I want to share with you my personal motivation for representing this extraordinary work of art. In order to understand my motivation for representing The Final Call, all you have to do is look at your condition before accepting Islam. Then look at the condition of our people. Look at your condition now after receiving the truth. Is it better than it was before you accepted Islam? I certainly hope so. Are you where you want to be in life? I can guarantee many of us who are struggling in life, even after receiving the truth, are struggling as a result of our own hands and actions.

It's amazing how fast a fire can burn out an entire forest once a single flame is ignited. We intend to set flames to ignorance and falsehood. Yes, we intend to hurl truth at falsehood until it knocks out its brains.

In the beginning was the Word. Every time you open someone's mind to truth, you close someone's mind to falsehood. Opening minds to truth does wonders for your spirit and self-esteem. I was taught that whenever you deliver the word of God to someone, sin gets erased off your record.

Another way to look at it is when you deliver the word of God to someone, you get grace and mercy put back on your "credit card" called life. Being "maxed out" is not a good feeling. The average Final Call Newspaper goes through the hands of about seven people. That means with one Final Call, you could touch more lives than you know. Couldn't you stand to get more grace and mercy from Almighty God Allah?

Don't we enjoy the feeling of getting a heavy burden uplifted from our conscience or knowing that rewards truly come with being responsible?

Representing The Final Call gives you that feeling of contentment you get after knowing an important job is finally completed. It literally feels likes a burden has been lifted from your back. Distributing The Final Call can give you the feeling of doing 1,000 good deeds. And true believing people, whose good deeds outweigh their bad deeds, deserve to enter into the kingdom of heaven.

Representing The Final Call Newspaper alone is the reason why I stay afloat with my struggle as I strive to be a "True Believer" and Faithful Follower of the Honorable Minister Louis Farrakhan.

In 2006, I was in a righteous Final Call competition in Chicago; and that righteous competition challenged me to distribute close to 500 Final Call Newspapers, (paper-for-paper) in one day. So mathematically, if the average Final Call goes through the hands of seven different people, by Allah's permission, I single-handedly was responsible for reaching 3,500 people in one day. And since the Final Call is the number one tool and minister of the N.O.I, I received an abundance of grace and mercy from Allah.

If I could do that in one day, what could YOU do in one week? All praises are due to Allah. But if I am not consistent, just as grace and mercy is credited, it could just as well be depleted. We must continue to do our part on any and every level that we possibly can to spread the truth that mentally resurrects the minds of our people. I do this with The Final Call Newspaper, which has the truth and fire that can burn down acres of ignorance.

All you have to do is ignite the flame by knowing the value of The Final Call Newspaper. Ask not what your Nation can do for you, but what you can do for your Nation. The fire we once had for Islam and our nation is being put out and replaced by our own personal agendas. And some of us are beginning to doubt and ask ourselves questions like, "What am I doing here? Where am I going in life?"

As our National Trainer and Assistant Supreme Captain, Grandmaster Anthony Muhammad puts it, we need to repent and refocus on the first work, and that is the resurrection of the mentally dead, or else we will be of the losers and suffer the consequence.

It reminds me of two Bible verses that I often read, Revelations 2:4-5. It reads, *"But I have this against you, that you have left your first love. Remember therefore from where you have fallen, and repent and do the deeds you did at first; or else I am coming to you, and will remove your lampstand out of its place-unless you repent."*

In the Holy Quran, Surah 103 entitled, Al-Asr (The Time), it reads: *"In the name of Allah, the Beneficent, the Merciful. By the time! – Surely man is in loss, Except those who believe and do good, and exhort one another to truth, and exhort one another to patience."*

Every time I read this surah, the thought comes to mind that unless one is patiently practicing to be a righteous servant of God, and doing good deeds on a consistent basis, there is chance for error. I cannot stress enough the importance to be consistent with your role as a Saviour. That's right, Saviour. When you deliver The Final Call Newspaper of the Nation of Islam to the people, this makes us Saviours.

Now think about the work of Almighty God Allah. Does Allah stop working because of bad weather or adversity? The answer is no. We have to make modifications. We have to prepare and adjust to the weather conditions, just like any military for combat. We have to be consistent with The Final Call distribution and representation of the number one minister of the Nation of Islam.

When you truly have a genuine interest in the people, your mind-frame is always on the deliverance of the people. Whether it's the idiot box (television), prison or your local neighborhood, it doesn't take much to see that the world of socioeconomics, freedom, justice and human equality aren't getting better; it appears to be getting worse. If we just look at the condition of Blacks in particular, it is apparent that the seeds planted during slavery have fully blossomed today. Division, religious turmoil, disease, poverty, self-hatred and bad health were adapted during our 400 years of servitude during slavery; and these negative effects have become our habitual daily routines all the way into today's modern society.

How did we fall from kings and queens in our own land into captives of a race produced from our own DNA? More importantly, how did we fall from a civilized people down to the bottom of the totem pole of civilization? My personal research traces back to slavery. Throughout the time of this millennium, my personal observation has proven that no other teaching has been more successful at reform and resurrecting the Black man or woman in America than the teachings of the Most Honorable Elijah Muhammad as taught to us by the Honorable Minister Louis Farrakhan.

Furthermore, The Final Call has all the elements to spark or ignite the consciousness of all who read it with an open mind. And those who read it with an open mind will become inspired to learn more about themselves and the time in which we live in and what must be done. Those who read The Final Call with an open mind will be confronted with checkmate truth that will force one to study and research for themselves. We as members of the Nation of Islam must always remember that our Sole Purpose is to deliver the 17 million or more mentally dead to the Lamb of God, the Most Honorable Elijah Muhammad. Never forget your sole purpose.

Next to the Honorable Minister Louis Farrakhan, The Final Call Newspaper is one of the most proficient ways to deliver any person with an open mind to Almighty God Allah.

"In the beginning was the word... and the word was made flesh." Every time an open minded person reads The Final Call Newspaper, seeds are planted. You don't see the plant the same day you planted the seed. This is why we are called Saviors, not salesman or paper boys. I would like to remind you that the Honorable Elijah Muhammad told us to look at the Minister. He told us to go where he says go, and to stay from where the Honorable Minister Louis Farrakhan advises us to stay away from. This is due to the great gift of vision and wisdom that Elijah Muhammad saw in the Honorable Minister Louis Farrakhan. For those of us who truly follow Elijah Muhammad's advice, and those of us who no longer doubt or question the Minister's vision, we are clearly on the straight path, and we too can benefit from his great gift and vision.

In the Bible, Matthew 10:24 emphasizes that the disciple is not above his teacher. If we look at the example that the Minister gives us in reference to both Master Fard Muhammad (God in Person) and the Most Honorable Elijah Muhammad, the Messenger of God, we clearly see that the Minister never makes himself equal to or greater than the Master nor his teacher. Yet, he continues to lead by example in everything he advises his students to do, including door-to-door Ministry. Take another moment and think over this.

In the book **Closing the Gap**, Brother Jabril Muhammad states: "From time to time, gaps develop as the leader moves ahead and the followers work to keep pace." He then goes on to expound upon a certain degree of misunderstanding that sometimes arises amongst some of the followers concerning the way the Minister relates to the broad community, including the Caucasian race. Out of the Minister's detailed and powerful response concerning the followers, he says "... Nevertheless, if they don't stay in constant submission; in constant obedience; in constant study; and in constant growth; then gaps will develop between the teacher and the student that will lead the student (sometimes) to be critical of the leader when the teacher grows beyond the particular need of that helper that motivated that helper to first want to help."

I get a plethora of epiphanies on many levels when I dissect the Minister's response to Brother Jabril's statement. One of them is, as the Minister grows to deliver the word of Almighty God Allah on a national and international level, ill or not, then we should at least be evolving as his helpers locally. After all, we signed the pledge cards saying that we believe. We signed the pledge card pledging to help. The Final Call Newspaper is the #1 tool of the Nation of Islam. We must amplify General Order #1. We MUST take charge of our post(s), and ALL temple property in view. After all this is OUR nation. Do Your Part.

Student Minister Nuri Muhammad (center) visits Student Minister Patrick Muhammad (Brother Nuri's Right) and The Mighty FOI of the 7th Region.

The Honorable Minister Louis Farrakhan said that, other than himself, The Final Call Newspaper is the number one minister of the Nation of Islam. Thus, it is important to represent the number one minister perfectly. According to Dictionary.com, the word "perfect" has 22 connotations to depict its meaning by way of adjectives, nouns and verbs.

As a verb, perfect means: to make fully skilled. As an adjective, perfect means accurate, exact, or correct in every detail: a perfect copy or thorough; complete; utter: perfect strangers. With these definitions in mind, we see that when Christ asks us to be perfect as he was; this goal is highly obtainable. The intent of this manual is to make us thorough, complete and fully skilled in representing the number one minister (next to the Minister) of the N.O.I; and that is The Final Call Newspaper.

I will confess that until I arrived at such a conviction to follow the Minister, I was truly one of the losers. I became homeless, living in a house that belonged to one of my brothers, which was to be sold. I became 50 pounds overweight. Let me explain it in a verse I wrote in a song called "Do Your Part" from my 2009 CD entitled "I Believe." The song is called:

Do Your Part

I came through the door

I said it before

I'll never let Iblis

Hypnotize me no more

Like when I signed that pledge card

Way back in '94

It's the truth! I know ... I know ...

I just didn't feel it no more.

See I was tired of fishing

And selling The Final Call

Broke my Word and my nerve

Then I started to fall

I saw hypocrisy

Like this is irrelevant

Used deceptive intelligence Swollen up like an elephant

Overweight I didn't pray,

I didn't fast no more

I was one who went astray

And felt the wrath for sure

Making excuses for my failures

When I really didn't try

Like I forgot the meaning

Of an F.O.I

See … I didn't abort the mission

It was in the back of my mind

For my personal grind

Broke General Order Number 9

I got a new mind now

This old mind I'm replacing

ACTIVE F.O.I until I die … for my nation

Just do your part, I'll do my part. We do our part … THIS IS OUR NATION!

Brother Hashim Hakim speaks to the FOI at Muhammad's Mosque #4 in Washington, DC

Another one of my motivations for distributing The Final Call Newspaper is that one can make a fairly decent living by making our communities a decent and safer place to live with The Final Call Newspaper. Keeping in mind that The Final Call Newspaper is dedicated to the resurrection of the Black man and woman of America and the world, with the title of Saviour, you can provide for yourself, your nation and your community all at the same time.

One of the responsibilities of good leadership is to always be thinking about the advancement of those whom you are trying to lead. In a meeting with our beloved and mighty Supreme Captain, Mustapha Farrakhan, I heard him explaining the pros and cons of increasing the cost of The Final Call Newspaper. While listening to him, I could gather that the decision to increase the cost of The Final Call Newspaper from one dollar to two dollars was not an easy decision. However, one of the contributing factors to that increase was that those responsible for distributing The Final Call will now get a one dollar profit whereas previously it was thirty cents. Let's do the math.

On May 4th, the Southern Regional Minister, Student Minister Abdul Sharrieff, challenged all student ministers and study group coordinators in the Southern Region, to lead by example pertaining to the enthusiasm and distribution of The Final Call Newspaper.

Although the challenge was accepted by various mosques and study groups in Mississippi, Alabama and Georgia, something very special happened in Knoxville, Tennessee. On the following week, May 11th, I personally wanted to do something very special during the 84th birth anniversary of our spiritual father, the Honorable Minister Louis Farrakhan.

Not only did I increase from 200 to 500 Final Call Newspapers this particular week, but in 8 hours and 40 minutes, I distributed 200 Final Call Newspapers in 84 degree weather in one day, by Allah's permission.

I wanted to know how many Final Call Newspapers I could distribute in 8 hours and 40 minutes. The Honorable Minister Louis Farrakhan's 84th birth anniversary fell on a Thursday and the F.O.I started at 8 a.m. that morning. At 8:15, it started raining.

There are always challenges when doing something great. So we just prayed and asked Allah to hold off the rain and in 15 minutes, it stopped raining (8:30 a.m.)

With proper hydration and multiple breaks, I finished my first bundle (100 Final Call Newspapers) at 1:30 p.m. And at 4:40 p.m., two bundles (200 Final Call Newspapers) were distributed to the residents of Knoxville, Tennessee from my hands alone. All praise is due to Allah.

I'm sure the Minister appreciates gifts and acknowledgements on his birth anniversary; however I'm even surer that he would love and appreciate knowing that those under his leadership are leading by example when it comes to the resurrection of our people and making our communities a decent and safer place to live.

Not only do I want to show my love and appreciation to the Minister for his dedication and sacrifice for the resurrection of our people, I wanted to show myself and others that if I could distribute 200 Final Call Newspapers in a day, what could we as grateful Believers do in a week? On the very next day, Friday, I distributed another 150 Final Call Newspapers by Allah's permission. On the very next day, Saturday, I distributed another 150 Final Call Newspapers by Allah's permission. To be clear, that's 500 Final Call Newspapers in three days. 500 Final Call Newspapers at two dollars each is one thousand dollars in three days. Think over that.

This is an exemplary way to show our Father that we are grateful, that we love him and that we appreciate him. Little did I know the weather would be 84 degrees in Knoxville, but at the end of day, it all made sense.

Brother Hashim Hakim poses with the 500 Final Call Newspapers he distributed

Mid Summary Questions:

What is The Final Call Newspaper?

1. What year was the original version of The Final Call Newspaper founded? What was it called? Who founded it?

2. What year did "The Final Call to Islam" evolve into "Muhammad Speaks"?

3. What was the weekly circulation of Muhammad Speaks? What was the monthly circulation?

4. The Final Call Newspaper as we know it today was founded by ______________________________ in the city of ____________________in_____________________.

5. According to the reading, what is the definition of the word "Saviour"?

6. What is your mission or Sole Purpose as a registered member in the Nation of Islam?

7. According to the reading, what is the definition of dead?

8. On an average, The Final Call Newspaper goes through the hands of about _______________ people.

9. What does the word perfect mean as a verb? And what does it mean as an adjective?

10. What is the definition cause?

4

The Seeds of the P.A.T.H.

Behold, in my hands rests the seeds of the P.A.T.H. With these seeds, you can attain the way of the Farmer and the Fisherman. With these seeds, you can accomplish what you will. The harvest you reap will benefit you abundantly; in ways that will pleasantly surprise you. The only thing that can hold you back is fear.

Do not plant these seeds if you have mischievous intentions. One must have a genuine interest in people and a sincere sense of community. If your objectives are selfish or your motives are to take advantage of the people or the Nation of Islam, I warn you that you are sowing dangerous seeds that breed failure. After all, what goes around is patiently waiting to come back around.

These seeds can literally save your life. Take them. Plant them. Live.

P.A.T.H. (Patience, Attraction, Technique, Humility)

Patience: The one who is consistent with prayer understands the unspoken power of patience, which is demonstrated by waiting for what you prayed for to become manifest without complaining. It's also the premeditated thought to carry out an action; or the visualization of a thought that becomes manifested with focus and meditation. This is done while you transmit thought from your mind into the universe. You produce the thought.

While you produce and cultivate the thought or idea, the higher powers of the universe go to work to make that idea a reality. Thought shapes reality and if you develop the science of bringing your thoughts into reality, you are experimenting with the power of God. For this to happen, one must have patience. As with planting any type of plant bearing seed, you don't see the rose the same day you plant the seed. However, if you continue to nurture the practice of patience, and thought, as long as you carry out the action, it is and will be obtainable.

Attraction: The one who has the power to attract, understands the effectiveness of imagery and appearance. Attraction power becomes effective the instant a person hears, sees, or observes you in action. Have you ever met a male or female who was attractive to you until they started talking? That should let you know that attraction oftentimes starts way before you speak. It is important to look extraordinary at all times. You never know who's watching you. Your presence alone should exemplify dignity, power and prestige. You must be well-groomed. You must smell, look, and dress extraordinarily attractive. I would even go so far as to say make manicures apart of your weekly routine. Do not take this seed for granted. The power to attract is a vital part of your approach. Your attire must be clean at all times. You must smell pleasant at all times. You must be well-groomed at all times. Never go in the public with soiled dirt in your clothing. Never go into the public with visible malfunctions in your clothing. We must inspect one another and want for each other what we want for ourselves. Guiding Rule of Conduct #4: We must be clean at all times (mind and body) at home and abroad. Never underestimate the unspoken power of attraction.

Technique: The one who has technique understands the need for versatility. There is a proper response for any person you come in contact with. Every word that comes out of your mouth is a contribution to the sale or no sale. Even non-verbal communication — facial expression, tone of voice, and gestures — are major factors. Furthermore, each of these elements can be either effective or ineffective. No action should be wasted. The more effective you are in using these elements, the more effective you will be in accomplishing your mission. Your tactic should be to either obtain a seed or a sale. Your strategy should be to win them over, one person at a time. And this takes practice.

Humility: The one who has humility understands the way of inheritance. The most resourceful element of the P.A.T.H. is humility. It is to be utilized at all times. Humility coupled with proper communication equals effectiveness. It is like pressure applied in a martial arts lock or hold. The more your prospect resists the more humility you apply. On the other hand, the moment your prospect submits, humility is toned down. Whatever it is you are trying to attain, the seeds of the (P.AT.H.) will help you accomplish it.

Chapter 4 Questions

1. What does the acronym of P.A.T.H. abbreviate?

2. One who is consistent with prayer understands the unspoken power of__________.

3. Define patience

4. Your presence alone should exemplify________ and _________.

5. Define attraction:

6. The one who has technique understands the need for _________.

7. Define technique:

8. The most resourceful element of the P.A.T.H. is ?

9. Define humility:

10. Humble means weak, afraid or lacking in strength. T/F

5

The Way of the Fisherman

The fisherman knows that depending on the type of fish he is trying to catch, there will be a need for various types of bait (techniques). An experienced fisherman knows what attracts the various types of fish (people). For example, bass like moving or sometimes shiny objects that appear to be alive. Bass, in this case, can represent a flashy or youthful person. Catfish like the exact opposite— a strong, dead, foul-scented type of bait. Catfish, in this case, could represent the poor, despised, and rejected or maybe even someone labeled to be beyond hope; someone caught up in the life of this world.

There are exceptions from time to time. For example, when a fish is hungry, it might eat anything. Islam comes after everything else has failed. We are living in a time when most will agree that everything has failed us as a people. The knowledge of what may be used to attract various fish comes from trial and error and through experimentation. This fishing methodology is what I use to attract people from all walks of life. And over the years, with the help of Allah, I have developed a mode of natural attraction for various scenarios through trial and error that would not have come to me otherwise.

I want to reiterate that one must have a genuine interest in the fish (people). If your objective is to take the fish out of the dirty water, scale, fry, and eat (take advantage of) the fish for yourself; I warn you that you are sowing dangerous seeds that will inevitably birth repercussions. Again, what goes around is patiently waiting to come back around. Do not use these seeds for mischievous intentions or to steal or take advantage of the people and your nation. The object is to take the fish out of the dirty water and place them into cleaner water (deliver them to the Messenger of Allah).

Brother Hashim Hakim poses with The F.O.I of Muhammad's Mosque #74

(From Far Left) Brother Theophilus Muhammad, Brother Hashim Hakim, (Back row) Brother Daniel, Brother Jason and Brother Ahmad. (Center) Brother Henry 2X, Brother Derreck "4Real", and Student Captain Terry Muhammad (Far Right)

Chapter 5 Questions

1. Depending on the fish you are trying to catch, there will be a need for various types of

______.

2. The knowledge of what may be used to attract various kinds of fish (people) comes from ______ and ______, through __________.

3. What are some things that can happen if you take advantage of the people (fish)?

4. Define repercussions:

5. What is the objective of the fisherman in the Nation of Islam?

6. Define genuine:

7. The Honorable Elijah Muhammad teaches us that "The Pearl" is in the fish's mouth. Explain.

8. According to Merriam-Webster, the definition of fisherman is "one who engages in fishing as an occupation or for pleasure." In your own words, reword the definition as it relates to inviting a guest to the mosque or Islam.

9. After redefining the word fisherman, do you consider yourself to be an effective fisherman for the cause of Islam and your nation? Why or why not?

10. Although The Final Call Newspaper is an effective tool for introducing a person to Islam or the mosque, your appearance and approach can determine whether a person purchases The Final Call Newspaper.

6

The Way of the Farmer

Study your terrain. Look at the condition of the people who inhabit the area or neighborhood you plan to cultivate. As a farmer, you should have three imminent concerns:

1. When to plant your seeds
2. Where to plant your seeds
3. How to plant your seeds

Metaphorically, if the soil is dry and crumbly, the seeds you plant won't develop properly without moisture. In other words, if the area or neighborhood you are working in is dark, desolate and crime-riddled, you have to bring light, activity and order utilizing the first two seeds of the P.A.T.H., Patience and Attraction Power.

So, if you are approaching a person that seems uninterested, stone-faced, or cold-spirited, the second two seeds (Technique and Humility) should be utilized first. This may be a simple "Have a nice day," "God bless you," or "I hope things get better for you, Brother/Sister." A kind gesture followed by a quick departure and onto the next field, person or prospect will go over well. This may take several attempts, days, months or even years to master without taking offense or showing emotion. Just remember do NOT take it personal. Over a period of time, you will have cultivated this person, bringing out of him/her a warmer response at the very least. Now you can implement the first two seeds of the P.A.T.H., Patience and Attraction Power.

I remember attempting to sell a brother The Final Call Newspaper and he cursed me out. I have to say, I was embarrassed and hurt. Although, I remembered to say "God bless you and maybe next time." I remember walking away a bit stunned. But I quickly recomposed myself, because I was in the public's view.

I continued to follow the P.A.T.H., and eventually forgot that even happened. It wasn't even 30 minutes later when that same person came. I didn't even recognize him. He said, "I apologize for going off on you like that. And what got me was when you said God bless you. I drove off thinking to myself, I need all the blessings I can get. " He purchased the paper and I was stunned a bit more when he apologized. (You have to trust me on this one. The P.A.T.H. works.)

Remember, you must have a genuine interest in what you are doing. More importantly, you must have a genuine interest in the person you are communicating with. If you find that the environment is hostile, let your Attraction Power intrigue the person. Time is of the essence. The more seeds you plant, the higher the conversion rate at harvest time. In other words, the more Final Calls you pour into a community, the better your chances of winning over a community.

While the seeds of the P.A.T.H. are planted, the process of cultivation is instantly underway. With the seeds of the P.A.T.H., your chances for winning over a community will increase rapidly.

Chapter 6 Questions

1. Define terrain:

2. What are three primary concerns of a farmer?

3. Define farmer:

4. Can the word farmer metaphorically be used to describe one who distributes The Final Call Newspaper, one who plants a seed or thought?

5. If the soil you are trying to plant seeds in is dry and crumbly, what are some challenges you might face?

6. If the area or neighborhood you are working in is dark, desolate and crime-riddled, you have to bring light, activity and order by planting which two seeds?

7. If you are approaching a person that seems uninterested, stone-faced, or cold-spirited what two seeds might you plant?

8. What is one of the tools that can help better your chances of winning over a community?

9. Define the word cultivate:

10. As it relates to our Sole Purpose of delivering the 17 million more mentally dead to the Lamb of God, the Most Honorable Elijah Muhammad, do you currently consider yourself to be an effective farmer?

7

Fear is an Illusion

Whenever we engage in a new activity, job, neighborhood or endeavor, there is a natural sense of discomfort due to the unknown variables of each situation we encounter. Before going any further, I feel that there should be something mentioned of fear. If you check the fear within, the fear without (others) can do you no harm. It starts with wandering thoughts and contemplative voices that breed skepticism concerning the unknown, or something inconceivable in our minds. These wandering thoughts and voices pose themselves as defense mechanisms. They are swift and aggressive. They seek out threats and failure in efforts to protect us...supposedly.

Fear is an illusion to the fearless, but to the fearful, it is the crippler of the potential conqueror in you. The Honorable Minister Louis Farrakhan teaches us to challenge fear if it arises. The mind is never unoccupied, and if you are not in control of your mind something else is; and oftentimes it is the entertaining of our negative thoughts and voices that develop into fear. With this in mind, this is an attempt to reestablish control of our mind and paralyze fear. You have the potential to be who or whatever you aspire to be. By the time you finish this chapter, you will be able to take charge of your mind and current situations regardless of how dark the situations may be, once you learn to challenge fear.

You should also be able to re-establish yourself back into the positive control you'll need to accept and be yourself. Practice and training are prerequisites for change. Consistency, on the other hand, implements the actual transformation of controlling your thoughts. Passion and desire alone won't make the change; you must practice, train, and remain consistent. When light shines, darkness vanishes. Sometimes we let the darkness from our past, coupled with the negative voices become us; thus we delay becoming what we were born to be.

In other words, we allow fear to dominate and restrict our lifestyles, and therefore, our true selves. When fear dominates, it assumes the position of power. We allow fear to sabotage our mission and goal. It restricts our ability to be honest for fear of how we may be viewed by others. Fear does not have faith in us, we have faith in fear. Fear does not have faith in us, yet we submit to fear like the once broken slave did to his master. We seek refuge in fear, yet fear has no sympathy for us. With all this said, I can confidently inform you that fear is an illusion.

Although fear appears to be an ally, it is the exact opposite in the end. There is no advancement towards our dreams and goals in fear. Fear keeps us in "was", thus, we never can advance to what "is" or what "can" be. It only exists if you allow it to.

Fear builds cumulative doubt in your ability to accomplish what you will. When weakness is detected, fear casts its veil of doubt. When doubt overshadows us, we become paralyzed and restricted from overcoming obstacles we may encounter in life. The illusion of fear will do whatever it takes to prevent you from succeeding. You overcome fear by challenging it. Once the practice of overcoming fear is developed, overcoming it again and again will be effortless. Know that fear is an illusion and unreal to the one who controls his/her mind with positive thinking and faith in Allah (God).

Fear is like any other obstacle; you must meet it head on in order to overcome it. The Honorable Minister Farrakhan says, "We must use faith to starve fear. He says fear has many different masks, and whatever you fear will become your master. Again, you overcome fear by challenging it."

When you feel fear creeping in, you counter the negative thought with prayer to God. You call on Him for His presence and power to help you crush the illusion of fear. In the book, **"Message to the Blackman**," under the subtitle of Truth, the Most Honorable Elijah Muhammad says: "It is a shame to see our people in such fearful condition." The Bible says in Revelations 21:8: "The fearful and the unbelieving shall have their part in the lake which burns with fire and brimstone which is the second death."

The Most Honorable Elijah Muhammad goes on to say in the same chapter, "The devil whom they fear more than Allah (God) was not able to protect himself against Allah; therefore, his followers shared with him the fire of hell." Under the subtitle, A House of Our Own in **Message to the Blackman,** the Most Honorable Elijah Muhammad says, "I say to my followers fear not! If you are with me, Allah is with you. And the more they attack us, the more Allah is attacking and will attack them. The truth of Allah will be universally and permanently established."

We must have faith and hold fast to what we say we believe, and who we say we follow. Again, practice and training are prerequisites for change. Consistency, on the other hand, implements the actual transformation of controlling your thoughts. Passion and desire alone won't make the change; you must practice, train, and remain consistent.

I want to confess to you that I was full of fear when I was first trained on how to represent The Final Call Newspaper. I was born in Aurora, Illinois; a rural suburb west of Chicago.

I lacked self-esteem. That was given to me by the Nation of Islam. I lacked purpose in life. That was given to me by the Nation of Islam. I lacked love and respect for myself and my people. That was given to me by the Nation of Islam. Despite attaining a new confidence in myself, and now knowing my purpose and this new love for myself and my people, I still was afraid to stand in the street and deliver The Final Call to those who wanted it.

I would hold The Final Call up from the curb and yell Final Call until I was hoarse; very ineffective when it comes to volume. As if I expected the people to get out of their cars at a green light and get the paper. I approached the cars timidly. This curb selling lasted 30 minutes before my lieutenant helped me to challenge my fear. The fear of walking up to complete strangers in a big city like Chicago was horrifying for me coming from the suburbs back in 1994. Not only did I have to initiate conversation with strangers, I had to stand in the busy streets of Chicago, and walk up to people I didn't even know. Now, I am fully driven as a Saviour. We must read each issue of The Final Call Newspaper in order to be in "The Know" and to explain and educate others on current topics and headlines in each issue.

What exactly was I afraid of? I was afraid of walking in traffic. I was afraid of going Door-To-Door. I was fearful in establishing business accounts. I was afraid that I did not know what to say to strangers. But most of all, I was afraid of being rejected. But thanks to strong leadership and qualified lieutenants who knew how to move The Final Call Newspaper by the bundles, I was able to emulate and reproduce myself over and over and over again in other brothers and sisters across the country. All praise is due to Allah.

The F.O.I consists of the truest brotherhood that I have ever experienced. And with proper handling, I was walking on water just like Peter. The difference is that I didn't sink. After my lieutenant pulled me in the street, he took me to the cars with him and told me to listen. And car by car he showed me with little effort how easy it was to represent The Final Call. I noticed he greeted everyone. He stated our cause and purpose. He was confident. He smiled when he received a donation, and he smiled when he didn't. When people said no, he thanked them and moved to the next car. When they said yes, he thanked them and moved to the next car.

It was important for me to see his poise, confidence and fearlessness. Shortly thereafter, in the same day, I caught the Holy Spirit, and distributed all 50 of my papers in a couple of hours. And I have fallen in love with the Mission of the Nation of Islam and The Final Call Newspaper.

As I learned to handle rejection, I began to prove to myself that fear was actually a big bully (smile). I must state that many will say no to the support of The Final Call, mainly because they don't know what it is. But more will say yes if you follow the seeds of the P.A.T.H. And when I heard the word "no", I transposed those to letters in my mind from NO to ON; which means "it's on" now.

I have to let the person know how powerful and useful the truth in this newspaper is. Initially, I used to ponder exclusively on the thought, how could someone reject something that literally saves lives and is good for you? I now have to say something worth remembering as they walk or drive off.

For example, "All that money we spend on Koreans, Arabs and White folks, God ain't good for $2?" Or I would break the ice by saying things like, "$2 donation to your own Black nation." Or "20 dimes, 40 nickels...or I'll even turn in 200 pennies if that's all you have." And right now, I know the reader is smiling, and so will the customer.

From that day on, I walked onto the field as if I was the man with the plan. "The doctor is in, have a seat." I want to thank every F.O.I from prior to 1975, and subsequent from those days for paving the way for us and the future. The Nation of Islam has a reputation of respect. And it is important that the F.O.I keep the legacy going. To do this, one must be persistent, fearless and consistent.

The point is, I conquered my fear by challenging it. We are sent to save our people. For we are not paper boys, we are Saviours. Do not appear to be afraid. Have you ever walked by a dog that was locked to a chain behind a fence and was still afraid? It's kind of funny when you think about it. But that's what it looks like when an F.O.I appears scared.

It really is an embarrassing sight to see. It is important to train and learn self-defense. No member in the Nation of Islam should be exempt of such training unless they have physical complications to prevent them from doing do. Martial arts and self-defense will increase your confidence that much more.

Chapter 7 Questions

1. Define fear:

2. According to the reading fear is an ________.

3. What does the Honorable Minister Louis Farrakhan advise us to do if we become fearful or if fear arises?

4. Fear is like any other obstacle; you must meet it head on in order to overcome it. T/F

5. Practice and training are prerequisites for ________.

6. Why should you read each issue of the Final Call?

7. Can you recall a moment when you challenged your fear and overcame it?

8

Prayer and Visualization

Referencing our Muslim Daily Prayer pamphlet, "The objective of prayer is the purification of one's heart, which is necessary for spiritual advancement. Allah promises many blessings to you if you turn to Him in prayer...Nations are destroyed when they indulge in EVIL inordinately, and they prosper so long as their good quality preponderate."

Prayer for me is an act of meditation and visualization. Whenever I desire something, I first take it to Allah (God) by visualizing a clear picture of what I am trying to obtain. But before I ask of what I desire, I go through a series of praising and giving thanks for what God has done and what He continues to do for me. I thank Him for His grace and mercy. I thank Him for waking me up every morning; for there are some that He calls back to Himself every second of the day. I thank Him for the faculties of hearing, tasting, smelling, seeing, hearing and others.

It is like trying to open a combination lock. There are a few steps that you have to take before you open the lock. First, you have to start at zero, which means you need a clear mind. Then you go to the right a few times, then left a couple times and back to the right and then the lock is open. It is the same with acknowledging God before you can open His vault of peace and blessings; you have to praise and thank Him. You are asking Him for what is already in existence, yet it is not yet in your possession; and this is where visualization comes into play. You must paint a clear mental picture of what it is you are trying to attain. If I say I'm going to sell 500 papers in a day, I would go to work visualizing how I would do it.

Visualization works on multiple levels. First, visualization works hand in hand with the second seed of the P.A.T.H., which is Attraction. How you see, think and carry yourself imposes an idea of who you are to others. On another level, visualization techniques stir up emotions that prompt you to carry out an action. When you are consistent with creating mental pictures of your image and your goals, you will be divinely motivated to carry out your goals and aspirations. The art of visualizing good mental pictures will have you motivated and feeling positive about your goals.

On a higher level, this divine motivation imprints the mental pictures with the positive attitude into your subconscious mind without any permission from you or the universe. It goes to work making those mental pictures a reality. The only reason you didn't obtain your goal is because you didn't work for it, or you gave up. Once you visualize the mental picture, your subconscious mind does the same. You are now on a promising journey of manifestation. What you are seeking is seeking you.

This is why it is important to use this wisdom for positive outcomes. Just as this knowledge can be used to assist, it can be used to hinder; and you may reap what you have sown.

Don't be alarmed like you don't understand it; what goes around definitely comes back. Most people are content with the comfort zone of being mediocre. They are content with fulfilling the visions of others rather than the visions of their own, even if their ideas are more effective. Anyhow, to be extraordinary, one MUST master the art of visualization. Every artist, architect, and inventor calls on their imagination.

To become extraordinary, you must visualize yourself being extraordinary. If you are going to do anything, do it and do it big. If you are consistent with your vision, it will become a reality.

First, visualize yourself doing it. Take notes on how you did it in your vision, and then just do it. Of all the study and research on visualization, what sticks out the most are Michael Jordan quotes. In his book, "For the Love of the Game," Michael Jordan says, "I visualized where I wanted to be, what kind of player I wanted to become. I knew exactly where I wanted to go, and I focused on getting there."

I challenge every person who reads this book to set a goal and focus on getting there. The focus comes from consistent visualization and mental pictures of you accomplishing what you set out to do first, and then bringing that thought to fruition by physically walking into your vision the same way you visualized it. The manifestation process is consistent so long as you are.

(A Soldier's Prayer)

A Special Prayer for Those on the P.A.T.H

Say: I seek refuge in you Allah from Shaitan, the Rejected enemy and the disbelieving people.

In the name of Allah, The Beneficent, The Merciful!

All praise is due to Allah, The Lord of The Worlds!

Oh Allah, I thank You for life after death and I will appear before You on the Day of Judgment in Your favor.

I thank You for allowing us to awake this morning, for there are some who did not. I am grateful.

Oh Allah! I ask You to loosen the knot in my tongue and give me a proper response for whoever I come in contact with on this day.

Help me to keep in mind that I am a Saviour first.

Help me to rise above my emotions.

Protect me from the enemy within and the enemy without.

Protect my family while I do this work.

Keep me on the path until I reach my goal.

I ask these things in the name of the Most Honorable Elijah Muhammad, the exalted Christ, the Honorable Minister Louis Farrakhan, our Divine Reminder, and You who appeared to us in the person Master Fard Muhammad. I am a helper in YOUR cause with YOUR Apostle. Please grant to me success.

Ameen

Chapter 8 Questions

1. What is the object of prayer?

2. What does prayer mean to you?

3. Before you ask Allah for anything, what should you do?

4. _______ is a key component of prayer.

5. Visualization works hand in hand with which seed of the P.A.T.H. and in which way?

6. Define visualization:

7. Define meditation:

8. When you are consistent with creating mental pictures of your image and your goals, you will be ____ ______________.

9. Most people are content with the comfort zone of being_______________.

10. Starting now set a weekly goal and begin to visualize how many Final Call Newspapers you will distribute. By Saviours' Day next year, how many will you have distributed?

9

Things You Must Know

Before ever stepping out to represent The Final Call Newspaper, there are a few things you must know and understand. First, you must study "The Time and What Must Be Done," an over 52-week series delivered by the Honorable Minister Louis Farrakhan. You must also remember 85% of the people are blind, deaf and mute about the times we are living in and what must be done to survive. Satan and his followers make up for 10% of the people who know and keep the Truth from the 85%. Then there is the 5% (Poor, Righteous Teachers) who are sent to deliver the Truth to guide and to warn the 85%. The members of the Nation of Islam represent this 5%. It is our obligation to deliver the Truth to our people.

These three categories of percentages cover the occupancy of man and mankind. So this should immediately make you aware that most of the people you encounter won't know the truth. Satan and his followers (10%) are doing their job in deceiving the people away from the truth that we are sent to deliver. Thus, the propagators of faith must repel the work of Satan with the teachings of The Honorable Elijah Muhammad as taught to us by the Honorable Minister Louis Farrakhan.

This means that most of the people will say "no" until we learn what it means to deliver a clear message. This means that we have to exemplify The P.A.T.H. and its meaning. This means that we have to make our presence felt in the community. This means that we have to make our presence felt in the world. And for those of us who have pledged to help in this cause, we have literally given an oath to God that we must uphold and fulfill, or else He is coming for us as stated in Revelation 2:5

The Duty of the Civilized Man – The duty of the civilized man is to teach and train the uncivilized.

Just as the Bible says in Romans 10 verses 14-15: *How then shall they call on him in whom they have not believed? And how shall they believe in him of whom they have not heard? And how shall they hear without a preacher? And how shall they preach, except they be sent? As it is written, how beautiful are the feet of them that preach the gospel of peace, and bring glad tidings of good things!*

Master Fard Muhammad reproduced himself in the Most Honorable Elijah Muhammad and countless others. The Most Honorable Elijah Muhammad reproduced himself in the Honorable Minister Louis Farrakhan and countless others. Likewise, the Honorable Minister Louis Farrakhan has and is reproducing himself in you and I and countless others. Thus, we too are responsible for carrying out their examples and the teachings of the Most Honorable Elijah Muhammad in the youth and countless others in America and the world. In that order.

We are sent to accomplish a mission, and that mission is to deliver the 17 million or more dead to the Most Honorable Elijah Muhammad. Of the various tools we have to use, The Final Call Newspaper is perfect.

"The business of The Nation is people. Teaching and training and qualifying people to handle people: That's our business..." ***The Honorable Minister Louis Farrakhan***

Chapter 9 Questions

1. What are three things one must know before stepping out to represent The Final Call?

2. What are the 3 percentage categories that cover the occupancy of man and Mankind?

3. Until we fulfill our obligation as the Poor, Righteous Teachers sent by God Himself, most people will say ___ to purchasing the _________.

4. What is the duty of the civilized man?

5. Martial arts and self-defense will increase your_________.

10

The Street Approach

There are four steps to this method. These four steps represent your foundation for attracting people to you and your movement. The street approach makes up for 60 percent of all distribution.

1. **THE GREETING**: Do not present the product, present yourself. This means that you greet the person with a handshake and a simple acknowledgement. A simple "How are you?" or "How are you feeling today King/Queen?" Notice the title I give the person. This name triggers an almost immediate boost in the self-esteem of the person(s) you are addressing. Once this is done, the person is more than likely willing to listen a little further to what you have to say.

2. **THE PURPOSE**: Explain to the person what you are trying to do. If The Final Call Newspaper is what you're distributing, you say something like this: "We are in the neighborhood attempting to make our communities a decent and safer place to live." Thought travels 24 billion miles per second. Do not bombard the person with a mission statement, especially at a stoplight. Try not to sound like a salesman. You don't want to give a pitch or presentation to a person who is trying to get to a destination in a hurry. Time is of the essence. Remember to be quick thinking, fast moving, right down to the modern times. We live in a faster paced society. Man was created impatient, so most people are impatient. You don't want to give the impression that you are selling something because selling takes time. You don't want to do a whole lot of talking when going door-to-door either. Stick to the script and answer questions to the point. Sound like a saviour who has come to help save the day.

3. **In straight words, say to the person what you want them to do.** Using The Final Call as the product, the technique is to point to the $2 on the front page of paper and say, "If this is too much for you, we are grateful for whatever God puts on your heart." Don't even think about it. Just say it exactly like that. I guarantee that you will see a drastic increase in distribution, volume and cash flow. You will also get blessed with donations that surpass $2. I get donations from $5 to $20 to $100 just about every time I represent The Final Call.

4. **Genuinely thank the person for their support!** This seems like common sense, but you'd be surprised at how many people forget to say thank you after getting a donation from someone they have just won over. People listen and remember those who thank them for their efforts. Be grateful.

Door - to - Door Approach (Business and Residential Accounts)

The four steps in the street approach also apply to the Door-to-Door method as well. These four steps represent your foundation for attracting people to you and your movement. The Door-to-Door approach makes up for 40% of all distribution. I would like to state that the ultimate goal is to move from the street to Door-to-Door and business accounts. The methodology for the Door-to–Door approach does not change except that you now have more time to dialogue. I should note here that it is very important to travel with someone who has good knowledge of both Bible and Qur'an. I can guarantee you that many folks will have questions of what the Muslims want and believe, and proper answers are just as penetrating to the mind of falsehood as are the seeds of the P.A.T.H. when representing the FCN.

People will wrestle with the truth for days, weeks and even months after you have had a discussion. I have also experienced parking lot distribution. This is where you sift Final Call patrons who are shopping in the strip malls and plazas. I should note here that whenever a person accepts or declines The Final Call Newspaper, you should hand them a flier or business card with your contact information. They may not have time or the money, but maybe they'd like to help, so hand them a card or flier. This is truly the essence of the P.A.T.H. being applied to the representation of The Final Call Newspaper.

11

FCNHD

Final Call Newspaper Home Delivery

"And everyone has a goal to which he turns (himself), so vie with one another in good works. Wherever you are, Allah will bring you all together. Surely Allah is Possessor of Power over all things."

Holy Qur'an 2:148

"You stand on the hot corners, but really what the Messenger wanted was [for] us to take the community and go door to door and get a customer. You'd be surprised what we'll find behind that door. Because there are many that we have touched with this teaching that has affected them and when you knock on the door and they see it's you, they'll take the paper and then you can ask them, 'Would you like to be a subscriber or may I bring the paper to you on a weekly basis?'

Then before you know it, you write their name down, you've got 5 customers, 10 customers, 15 customers, 30 customers, 50 customers, till you get to 100. Then one day you go back and you say, "Mrs. Jones, have you ever tried the Supreme Bean Pie?" ...And the next thing you know, we've got an army that don't even work for the devil anymore, because we're making money just with the products of the Nation of Islam!"

The Honorable Minister Louis Farrakhan

In a strategic meeting with Brother Glenn, the Assistant to our Mighty Supreme Captain Brother Mustapha Farrakhan, and our beloved Assistant Supreme Captain Grandmaster Anthony Muhammad, we designed and laid out the blueprint for The Final Call Newspaper Home Delivery. Brother Anthony thought of the name FCNHD, and we loved it.

WHAT IS HOME DELIVERY?

- **Customers secured via 10-week prepaid orders delivered by FOI** (not the Post Office).
- **Price: 10-week prepaid order for $24**
- **Billing automatic & recurring**
- **Prepaid orders count towards the City and Individual's FOI Orders**
- **The FOI Salesman secures his commission for each Final Call Newspaper with Home Delivery prepaid order.**

WHY 24 ???

- **Pricing Scale mimics current National Subscription Costs**
  - 50 Issues → $120
  - 10 Issues → $24 ($120 ÷ 5)
- **Revenues shared with all parties involved.**

Price Breakdown

- **$10 The Final Call**
- **$7 Believer (FOI)**
- **$3 Delivery FOI**
- **$4 Administration**
  - Database Mgmt.
  - Sales & Delivery Teams
  - National Staff
  - Local Captain.

- **$24 Total Price**

HOW WILL PAYMENT BE COLLECTED?

How will FCNHD work? Our sales force will knock on doors asking our people to help the **Honorable Minister Louis Farrakhan** to do for self and rebuild the wasted cities. We **will ask for 10 weeks of home delivery for a donation of $24 dollars that will automatically re-bill every 10 weeks unless we are told to end home delivery.**

We will take donations with our smart phones. The repeat billing will be through a 3rd party that specializes in card transactions.

What happens when a customer is re-billed? It will be as if that same Believer that fished the customer in had made a new sale. Meaning that as long as that customer remains a customer, the Believer will continue to get the coin from the fish's mouth.

Why are we using electronic payment methods?

We want to alleviate potential problems with theft and the mismanagement of the customers' money and the Believer's money.

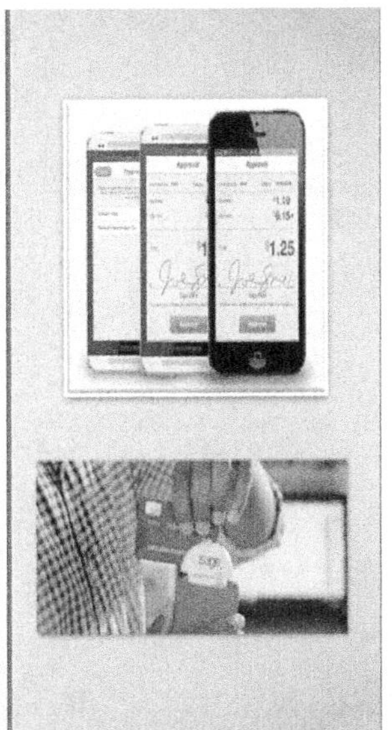

FINAL CALL NEWSPAPER
DOOR TO DOOR FLYER

The Final Call

10 WEEK HOME DELIVERY OF THE FINAL CALL NEWSPAPER $20

Customer Info

Name:

Address:

Phone:

Email:

Representative Name: Nation ID#

DOOR TO DOOR SCRIPT

- **Greetings my name is (your name) Hashim Hakim and I am a part of The Nation of Islam's (10,000 Fearless initiative, or Community Development initiative, etc)** and our aim and purpose is to make our communities a decent and safer place to live.
- Under the (instructions, commands or guidance) of **The Honorable Minister Louis Farrakhan** we are genuinely committed to the resurrection of our people in America and all over the world.

- Nationwide we are engaging, embracing and strengthening our communities with presence, conflict resolution intervention, and economic empowerment.
- **To help fund our efforts, we are offering a 10 week home delivery of The Final Call Newspaper for only $24.**
- On behalf of **The Honorable Minister Louis Farrakhan**, we would like to thank you for your time, consideration and efforts in making our communities a decent and safer place to live.
- Your servant in this cause,
- Brother Hashim Hakim (your name)

GOALS & BENEFITS

- **The Home Delivery system is the way we want to go.**
- **Our Goal is to make Final Call HD the primary method for the sale and distribution of the Final Call Newspaper.**
- **Engagement with Community**
- **Customer / People focused Effort**
- **Dependable Product Sales**
- **Improved Quality door-to-door Fishing**

"And say, Work; so Allah will see your work and (so will) His Messenger and the believers. And you will be brought back to the Knower of the unseen and the seen, then he will inform you of what you did."

Holy Qur'an 9:105

FROM THE OFFICE OF THE SUPREME CAPTAIN

Special thanks for all those who assisted with this presentation and initiative:

- Assistant Supreme Captain Anthony Muhammad — Chicago, IL
- Bro. Hashim Hakim — Detroit, MI
- Bro. John Muhammad — Fort Worth, TX
- Bro. Kosala X — Houston, TX

Furthermore, you can ask the store owner to let you do a trial run with 10 papers at their location, just to see how it goes for a couple of weeks. You have to be consistent, prompt and enthusiastic about the trial run. This will help inspire the owner to take a chance. Some things that can help your presentation are paper stands and signs of various sizes that promote The Final Call with your personal information on the signs.

Here are the five types of accounts that you should have set up:

1. Subscriptions by mail
2. Home delivery (residential)
3. Business accounts: gas stations and local businesses
4. Newspaper stands
5. The corner

"So, brothers, you can see we've got a lot of training to do. And so we organize, and we go after our people in a systematic way: block by block, street by street, house by house.

We knock on any door; just like He (Master Fard Muhammad) went, we go. And don't go ugly. Put your best foot forward.

And that's why, brothers, when people write about the followers of the Messengers they say they are clean, they are courteous, they are respectful, they are submissive, but underneath all of that they see that this is a dangerous body if ignited in that way. So this is going to be a balanced training."

The Honorable Minister Louis Farrakhan

12

Take Care of Your Feet

The foot is actually a very delicate structure. The areas of the feet have to support the entire body's weight as well as provide the motions required for us to move. Because of this, the foot can be very easily injured. The foot muscles and ligaments can become serious problems in one's life. I can recall the severe pain that came with my case of plantar fasciitis. The plantar fascia is the tendon that helps connect the bones on the bottom of the foot. The plantar fascia is easily inflamed by repetitive stress—caused by walking, running and the weight of your body. **Figure 1**

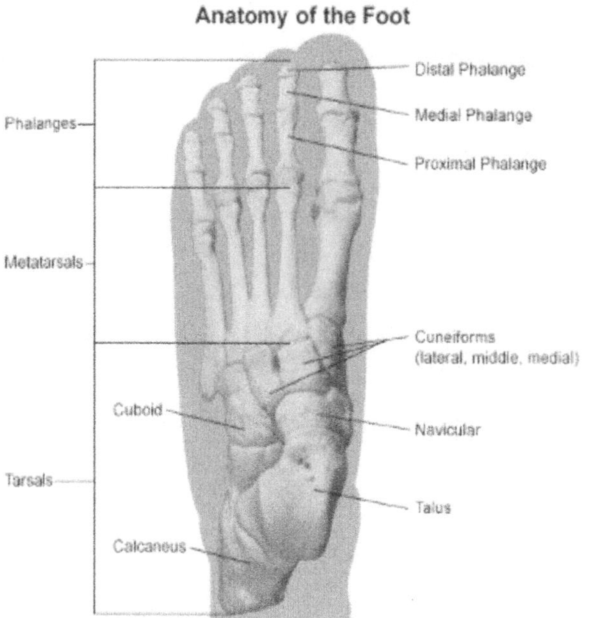

The foot is one of the most complex parts of the body, consisting of 28 bones connected by numerous joints, muscles, tendons, and ligaments. The foot is susceptible too many types of injuries. Foot pain and problems can cause pain and inflammation, resulting in limited movement and mobility.

Figure 1

Did you know that nerve damage can cause you to lose feeling in your feet? Sometimes you may not feel particles inside your socks that may cause sores on your feet. You may not feel a blister because of poor fitting shoes. Foot injuries such as these can cause ulcers which may lead to amputation. **Keeping your blood sugar in good control can also contribute to taking care of your feet and help you avoid further complications.**

Thin soled dress shoes and walking can literally be the “Achilles Heel” of soldiering. I recommend a ¼ inch to ½ inch rubber bottom sole; preferably with air or cushioned insoles. Wearing the wrong shoes can give you heel, knee, and back pain that can lead to more severe health problems like plantar fasciitis, and fallen arches etc. **Figure 2**

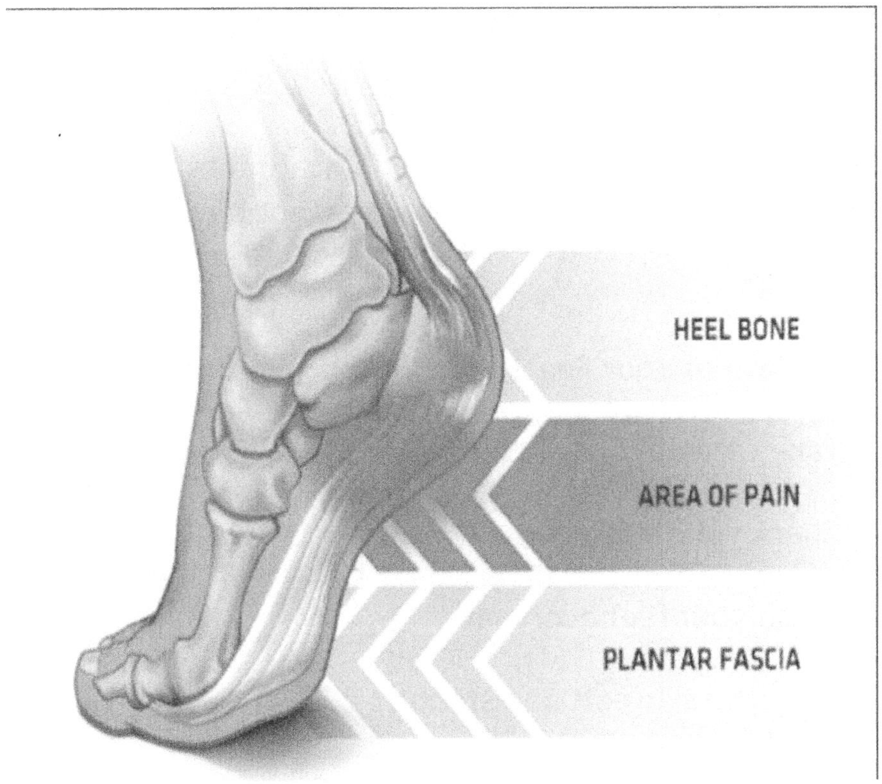

Figure 2

I have encountered all of the above. I was NOT able to work for several weeks and when you only have one stream of income, two or three weeks with no pay can really set you back.

Be especially watchful for:

- Numbness and loss of feeling in your feet.
- Changes in the shape of your feet.
- Foot ulcers or sores that do not heal (consult your physician).
- Foot ankle and leg swelling may indicate that there may be heart related issues that you may not be aware of.

Take Care of Your Feet!

1. Take care of your diabetes

2. Check your feet everyday

3. Wash your feet everyday

4. Keep the skin soft and smooth

5. Smooth out corns and calluses gently

6. Trim your toenails each week or when needed

7. Wear shoes and socks at all times

8. Protect your feet from hot and cold

9. Keep the blood flowing through your feet

If you have any of the problems discussed in this chapter, consult your physician.

13

...And Be His Peace

By A'ishah N. Muhammad

There's hardly anything more majestic and satisfying than the consolation in a man's soul from the peace his wife gives him. When he is doing the works of his Father in the Resurrection and delivering the mentally dead to the Lamb of God, her appreciation and support is as a healing elixir that gives his mind solace and rest.

"He created the woman that the man might find peace and quiet of mind in her. He made her as consolation for him."
The Honorable Minister Louis Farrakhan

The woman is Allah's Second Self. Within her is the desire to be most pleasing to her Lord and through her M.G.T Class, she is empowered and amply qualified in being her husband's peace. She understands the plight of the Black man and the many challenges he faces in a world that diametrically opposes God.

Every time he departs from home, he is entering Satan's battlefield where the chance of him being beat down, rejected, despised and even slain for standing firm in Truth, is heightened. Knowing what the Black man would face, Allah put in the woman's nature, comfort and consolation that would ease his troubles and bring calm to his spirit. Peace is a mercy from Allah.

"He that findeth a wife, findeth a good thing and obtaineth favor of the Lord." Proverbs 18:22

Peace is the freedom from disturbance; quiet and tranquility. It is the freedom from or the cessation of war or violence.

It is incumbent that his peace is protected so that he may have the spirit to build and work cheerfully in establishing the kingdom of God. The wife's role is to be that comfort and as long as her mind is aligned with Allah's through prayer, study, and a willingness to serve in accordance to His Will, peace can be sufficiently maintained.

To sustain peace, Allah should always be at the forefront of the wife's heart and the way of her devotion. She respects her husband and is submissive to him; just as he is obedient and submissive to Allah. She is pleasing to his eyes, attentive to his small desires and needs, studies what he likes, his dislikes and what he absolutely loves. She is a praying woman, soft-spoken and understands the importance of speaking life into her man, without fail.

Every morning for Fajr, they should awake and pray as one. After prayer, conjoin in Quranic reading and spiritual dialogue. It's the little meaningful things like serving him the Messenger's coffee or tea during his study that adds to his appreciation. She keeps him intrigued with stimulated high conversation, discussing the Life Giving Teachings, current world events, history and Nation Building. He loves when she asks questions for his insight. In truth, she is equally fascinated by his mind as he is hers.

The thoughtful things she does for him mean so much to him like:

*Preparing his meals at the proper time in accordance with How to Eat to Live, skillfully. Her being a scientist in her kitchen ensures his dinner is balanced with quality nutrition, healing, love and supreme sustenance.

*Welcoming him home with warmth, a smile, a kiss and being accommodating to his needs, especially after a long push.

*Making certain the children are exceptionally kept, well-groomed, educated, mannerable and respectful.

*Maintaining an immaculately clean home at all times.

*Keeping his flaws in confidence. We should never be highlighting his faults to others, belittling or humiliating him to anyone. She finds the best parts of him and settles there.

*Writing love notes and leaving them under his pillow, in his Qur'an, or in his sock drawer. Sending ayats via text throughout the day and packing him a thermos filled with delicious creamed navy bean soup when he soldiers, increasingly in the brutal winter months.

*Looking appealing, staying physically fit and sweet-smelling, keeping hair well-maintained and garments fashionable and refined.

*Giving special care to laundering and pressing his white shirts, also, dry cleaning his suits. Knowing how to sew and repair missing buttons or seams that fall out of place is priceless. When he looks the part by his wife's hands, he can perform his duty confidently and worry-free.

*Soaking his feet in a detox bath with tea tree oil and warm water, washing his feet with clay soap and scrubbing the stress out of his soles and heels with a pumice stone to smooth the blisters. This is quite relaxing after soldiering hard.

*Learning and mastering the art of reflexology. Massaging peppermint essential oil with almond or jojoba oils in his beautiful Black skin, this expression is extremely therapeutic to him.

*Being spontaneous; never becoming mundane or predictable. Always keep the feminine mystiques captivating to him.

*Random back and shoulder rubs. He works very hard and this is so rewarding to him.

*Public and private praise. Uplifting him in the eyes of others speaks volumes of her admiration for him. She should compliment what she loves about his mind, body and soul.

*Knowing when to step back to allow him personal space and freedom.

Sometimes he needs to regroup and realign with Allah and she absolutely must respect that.

*Setting aside special quality time to be uninhibited in exploring the art of intimacy, Sacred Touch, and Tantra. This is vital for the longevity of the fire to remain ALIVE in the marriage. It is also consoling to the physical needs of both the husband and wife. Communicating desires and constantly discovering new ways to activate the intimate love is critical. The bond it produces is otherworldly!

*Take time to learn him. Be open in trying new adventures with him keeping within the law. Hug him often. Kiss him passionately. Cater to him in righteousness. Be kind and submissive. Make the home an oasis; a refuge of serenity.

...and this is how to be his peace.

A'ishah N. Muhammad

14

On Any Given Day

Taking into consideration that I have set my weekly goal, my mental preparation for propagating the faith starts the night before. Depending on the vehicle of distribution, whether you have business accounts, FCNHD, or the street corner (F.O.I only), the weekly goal for every able-bodied Believer should be at least 100 FCN per week. There are 168 hours in a week, and the question each of us must ask ourselves is, "How many hours will I need to accomplish my weekly goal of 100 Final Call Newspapers?"

Business Accounts:

1. 10 businesses that carry 10 FCN in each of their stores.

1. You will need an 'FCN SOLD HERE' sign.
2. The business gets $0.50 per issue for carrying your paper. Simple, right?

FCNHD: Your 100 FCN will be sold in advance for 10 weeks. You are responsible for guaranteeing that your customer receives their Final Call Newspaper each week.

1. 10 door-to-door customers that pay you $24. They are paying for 10 weeks of The Final Call Newspaper in advance. (See FCNHD chart for details.)
2. Order you FCNHD kit (Please see contact information at the end of the book.)

The Corner (F.O.I only): Implementing the P.A.T.H., each brother is to distribute at least 25 FCN per hour. This depends on the demographics of your city, and the legal ramifications of whether you are permitted to distribute FCN in your city. This should take at least four to five hours at the max. I would suggest you bring our Propagation Team to your city for a seminar. (See contact information)

SAVIOURS' DAY
2PM FEB 17

I wake up with Fajr prayer and I pray for the power, will and strength to accomplish my goal. I partake in some Quranic reading and/or listen to clips of the Minister to clear the air for the day. This is my favorite clip prior to soldiering: https://www.youtube.com/watch?v=LoXiYWNnL44&t=134s .

Oftentimes I will take post quotes from The Holy Quran and/or the Minister on social media that stood out to me such as:

8:29 *O you who believe, if you keep your duty to Allah, He will grant you a distinction and do away with your evils and protect you. And Allah is the Lord of mighty grace.*

The Holy Quran (Maulana Muhammad Ali translation)

I might even partake in light calisthenics. And before you know it, I'm focused on being as attractive as I can possibly be, appearance wise. From my haircut to the shine on my shoes, everything is on point. By this time, my phone is ringing and the brothers are en route to the field. We thrive off righteous competition. On this particular day, Brother Bilal, Brother Jamell and I decided to do a 9 a.m. to 5 p.m. on a Saturday. I might add, the brothers had not been in the ranks very long. So they walked right in to this kind of training. Take a look at their results. (See figure 3)

We started out at one particular location and the traffic was light. Our numbers were low. We recorded it. Then we moved to another location and the numbers were still low. We recorded it. So we decided to move to a third location and the traffic was just right. This may have been due to the early time that we started. Nonetheless, hour after hour up until 6 p.m., we recorded our numbers and this is how the day ended. (See figure 4)

Figure 3 Brother Bilal, Brother Hashim, Brother Jamell of Jacksonville, FL

Figure 4 Hourly report for Saturday

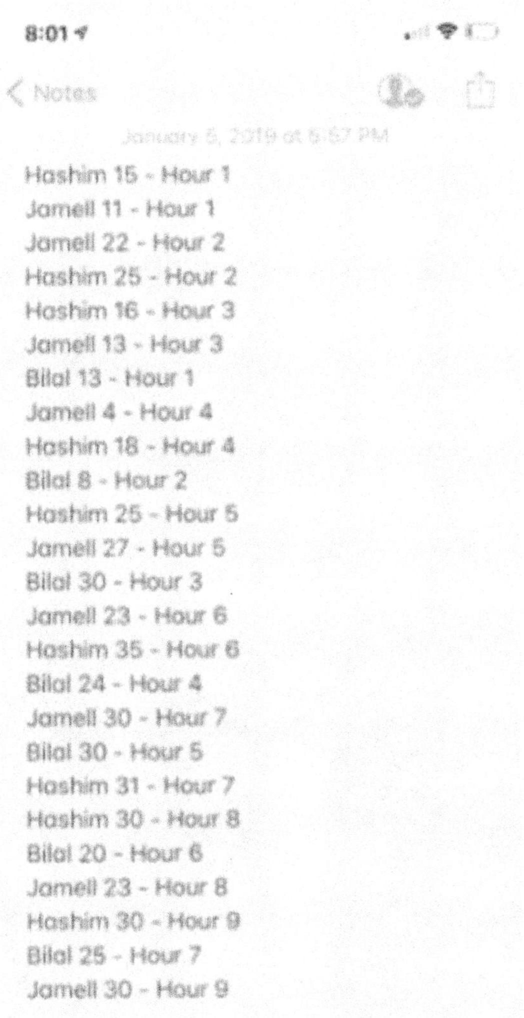

8:01

< Notes

January 5, 2019 at 6:57 PM

Hashim 15 - Hour 1
Jamell 11 - Hour 1
Jamell 22 - Hour 2
Hashim 25 - Hour 2
Hashim 16 - Hour 3
Jamell 13 - Hour 3
Bilal 13 - Hour 1
Jamell 4 - Hour 4
Hashim 18 - Hour 4
Bilal 8 - Hour 2
Hashim 25 - Hour 5
Jamell 27 - Hour 5
Bilal 30 - Hour 3
Jamell 23 - Hour 6
Hashim 35 - Hour 6
Bilal 24 - Hour 4
Jamell 30 - Hour 7
Bilal 30 - Hour 5
Hashim 31 - Hour 7
Hashim 30 - Hour 8
Bilal 20 - Hour 6
Jamell 23 - Hour 8
Hashim 30 - Hour 9
Bilal 25 - Hour 7
Jamell 30 - Hour 9

Every student captain and student minister should acknowledge the top salesman at every meeting.

Remember what the Most Honorable Elijah Muhammad said: ***NOTE TO THE MINISTER***: *Our newspaper is very important. I am charging you with the responsibility of instilling in the followers at your Mosque, the spirit to put a successful effort into our own.*

(From left to right) Brother Tony,. Brother Kareem, Brother Ke'Aundre, Brother Leandre and Brother Dawud of Muhammad Mosque #29

15

Our Way of Devotion

I called our Headquarters in Chicago to speak with Brother Glenn Muhammad. He is the assistant to the Supreme Captain, Brother Mustapha Farrakhan. I heard our first-rate, virtuoso, Supreme Captain say that if it were not for Brother Glenn, he could not do what he does for our nation. And every time I speak with Brother Glenn, I get inspired while brainstorming on subjects that deal with problem solving, numbers, quotas and goal setting.

This time, I called to inform him that The P.A.T.H. 2 was finished and ready for print. And in that discussion, I asked him, "is there a quota or goal per believer on recruiting each year?" Neither one of us recalled that information. So I asked him if I would be in error to implement that each able-bodied Believer should be able to recruit at least one Believer each year. He responded, "No Sir! This is our way of devotion."

And it was at that moment that I realized, there needed to be another chapter added to this book. This is where I want each of us to block out all distractions while reading this section. For this is what it's all about.

I have made the claim that it is very difficult to teach, show and inspire someone to do what we ourselves do not know how to do. It is very difficult to teach, show and inspire someone to do what we ourselves have not had a record of doing, or are not doing ourselves. Especially at this present time...

I humbly say this in the spirit that these verses are written in The Holy Quran*:*

In The Name of Allah, The Beneficent, The Merciful

2:44 Do you enjoin men to be good and neglect your own souls while you read the Book? Have you then no sense?

2:45 And seek assistance through patience and prayer, and this is hard except for the humble ones,

2:46 Who know that they will meet their Lord and that to Him they will return.

In Surah 2:44, we are asked "*Do you enjoin men to be good and neglect your own souls while you read the Book?*

Let us clear the word neglect:

ne·glect
/nəˈglekt/

verb

1. 1.
   fail to care for properly.
   "the old churchyard has been sadly neglected"
   synonyms: fail to look after, fail to care for, fail to provide for, leave alone, abandon; More

noun

1. 1.
   the state or fact of being uncared for.
   "animals dying through disease or neglect"
   synonyms: disrepair, dilapidation, deterioration, shabbiness, disuse, abandonment; *rare desuetude*
   "the whole place had a hopeless air of neglect"

As a verb, when something is not cared for properly, that is a form of neglect. Yes, there are levels to neglect, but what is more detrimental than neglecting our own souls? And how do we look trying to teach a subject(s) that we are not knowledgeable of; nor are we the example of? Have you then no sense? (Looking in the mirror)

As a noun, many of our mosques and study groups are in the state of being uncared for. It is mainly because of our failure to adhere to and carry out our Sole Purpose. And according to the Honorable Minister Louis Farrakhan, we have flatlined, which means we have failed to increase.

Let me reiterate that the Honorable Minister Louis Farrakhan has revealed to those of us who propagate the faith with The Final Call Newspaper, that we are doing the work of a minister:

*"Let me personally thank the F.O.I. who go out from their homes with The Final Call Newspaper, to bring the Message of the Most Honorable Elijah Muhammad and his Minister to the people. The Final Call is a wonderful newspaper, filled with knowledge and wisdom. Every newspaper is really a small book. So when you take The Final Call, and study it, and then deliver it to our people**, you are doing The Work of a minister**. You should not fear to go out amongst our people to deliver The Message; for The Bible says in (1 Chronicles 16:22) [Touch not mine anointed, and do My Prophets no harm.]*

You are walking in the footsteps of the Prophets of God. And even though you may be evil spoken of, even though you may be rejected, even though sometimes we are attacked, yet, we are following in the Footsteps of the Prophets of GOD. There is no nobler task in this world than to imitate and emulate the Prophets of GOD. You are with the One Who ends all of the prophets, and ushers in the World of GOD Himself."

The Honorable Minister Louis Farrakhan

Hence the words that are underlined; ***you are doing the Work of a minister.***

Now, bear with me as I bring this to a close. In "**The Restrictive Law of Islam Is Our Success"** book in chapter 8: **Acceptance of Our Universal Mission**, there is a subtitle**, Level of Productivity Determines the Success of the Business.**

"There's a disease in some of us in The Ministry, where the "need' for money literally has killed The Spirit of The Mission!" Remember those of us who deliver The Final Call Newspaper to our people are doing the work of a minister.

He goes on to say "These must work hard, and get after the Lost-Founds — that is The Nation! It's not selling bean pies; it's not selling The Final Call Newspaper. The Business of The Nation is people! Teaching and Training and Qualifying people to Handle people: That's our business. But The Nation has flatlined."

In context, he explains in the previous paragraph that the subject matter of some student ministers is not attracting the Lost-Founds to believe and follow through. I want to focus on the word attracting, which is what the "A" in The P. A.T.H. stands for. Remember, if the bait is NOT attractive, why would the fish bite? Furthermore, if we did attract them, did we attract them long enough to "believe and follow through?"

In the very next subtitle on page 151, **Knowledge and Acceptance of Islam as a Mission,** he states:

Now I want to ask a question: Is the acceptance of Islam the acceptance of a "religion," or, is our acceptance of Islam the acceptance of a Mission?

If we say it is the acceptance of a religion without a mission involved, indeed, then, this is a religion as we have always known "religion." A religion where people come to worship God, but there's no mission attached, then we're a "church": Where people come to pray, give in charity and try to observe church rules and work to maintain and increase their standard of living without a social responsibility.

However, Master Fard Muhammad, The Great Mahdi-Allah In the Person—showed us our way of devotion by attaching to our Islam The Mission of the Resurrection of the Dead. He demonstrated this for 3 and ½ years among us, and He gave this Assignment, Or Mission, to one who had the heart, mind, soul and spirit to accept such a weighty assignment. And The Saviour said to him: "Brother, you have the hardest job of any man that ever lived."

I had a discussion with an F.O.I who lived in the city of Jacksonville, FL before I moved there. And like many of us, our papers would be stacked in our garage, at the mosque or in the trunks of our vehicles. After Allah blessed me to train him, he would distribute his 100 Final Call Newspapers every week. He eventually increased to 150. All praise is due to Allah.

Again, by Allah's permission, I was blessed to have the opportunity to train this particular brother in The P.A.T.H., and at a certain point in his development, he felt he could take it from there in his training. I noticed he would change the language of The P.A.T.H. and when I stood him up to be an example of The P.A.T.H. to other men, he would start his talk like this, "Well what 'I' say is this that and the other."

I noticed his Final Call Newspapers began to stack up again as they were before his training began. He began to soldier on his own, whereas I teach it is better to soldier with the brothers as a unit. And just as some of us feel we have outgrown the Teachings of the Most Honorable Elijah Muhammad as taught to us by the Honorable Minister Louis Farrakhan, some of us take what we can from others and deem that we can do it better than our teacher, or act as if we are self-taught. I'm admonishing you, the reader; do NOT change The P.A.T.H.

Well, one day, there was a heated discussion. I asked him, "How is it that I just moved here, and by Allah's permission, I was able to recruit one of the most productive F.O.I in the entire 7th Region right here in your city? And why haven't others who were here before me done so?" And as if there was a breakthrough, he paused and said, "Be patient, it's coming."

We ended our discussion by giving each other the greetings and going our separate ways. Later that day, he called me to thank me for our conversation. He said it motivated him to be better.

And approximately one month later, this particular F.O.I fished in a married couple that is now in active training. The next time he came to soldier with me, I thanked him and told him, "That is what it's all about." All praise is due to Allah.

Now, I am not sharing this for vain purposes. I wanted him to look past our differences and look at what I am doing with The Final Call Newspaper. Like the Minister says, "These must work hard, and get after the Lost-Founds — that is The Nation! It's not selling bean pies; it's not selling The Final Call Newspaper. The Business of The Nation is people! Teaching and Training and Qualifying people to Handle people: That's our business. But The Nation has flatlined."

When I am present in a particular city and I am allowed to train in a manner that I deem and have proven to be effective, there will be outstanding results.

By Allah's permission, remember what we did in St. Louis at Mosque #28, under Student Minister Donald Muhammad and Student Captain John Muhammad? In 2012, The F.O.I superseded Chicago at times and that team was lead by high school students (hint). These brothers are now finishing college and I pray they come home and help the Minister and their Nation go to the next level with The Final Call Newspaper and recruitment. (See Figure 5)

Figure 4 Brother Akil, Brother Al Shareef, Brother Malik of St. Louis

By Allah's permission, remember what we did in Philadelphia under Student Minister Rodney and Student Caption Anthony? Remember what Allah blessed us to do in Detroit under Student Captain

Emeritus Roy? And those that were in my squad were doing 34% of the total number of FCN sold in Detroit. (See Figures 6- 7)

1	DETROIT, MI	5,700
2	WASHINGTON, DC	5,200
3	NEW YORK , NY	5,000
4	CHICAGO, IL	4,400
5	ATLANTA, GA	4,000
6	PHILADELPHIA, PA	3,700
7	LOS ANGELES, CA	2,800
8	NEWARK, NJ	2,100
8	HOUSTON, TX	2,100
9	BROOKLYN, NY	2,000
10	BALTIMORE, MD	1,700

Figure 6 Detroit Totals 2015

Volume 34, Number 45			
	NUMBER ONE MICHIGAN GOD SQUAD	INITIAL	FCN 1978
1	**Bro. Hashim Hakim**		350
2	Bro. Allen X		
3	Bro. Chris		100
4	Bro. Darrick A. Muhammad		
5	Bro. Darryl X		100
6	Bro. Ibrahim Muhammad		100
7	Bro. Jamel X		100
8	Bro. Kenneth 4X a.k.a. (Salih)		138
9	Bro. Kenneth (124073)		430
10	Bro. Kevin 3X		[illegible]
11	Bro. Terrell X		100
12	Bro. Trayvon (Proc)		50
13	Bro. William A. X (White)		210
14	Bro. William 3X		300
15			
16			

Figure 7 God Squad Totals in Detroit (2015)

Now, here lies the problem: When I leave the city, the spirit, energy and the numbers go down. So in discussing this dilemma with our masterful Assistant Supreme Captain, Grandmaster Anthony Muhammad, he explained to me that I was not properly reproducing myself. He explained how his students go on to be teachers, opening schools and recruiting other students to their schools. Thus, VSK is expanding vastly even outside of The Nation of Islam per say, even into other nationalities. We have a solution:

Propagation Officer

Post Position:

☑ Positioned below First Officer

☑ Equal in rank to the Lieutenant

PURPOSE

The Propagation Officer is tasked with the assignment of insuring that all of the men in the F.O.I are participants in the sale and distribution of The Final Call Newspaper. The Propagation Officer is more commonly referred to as the Paper Captain.

POST DESCRIPTION

The Propagation Officer works in concert with the lieutenants and squad leaders to strategically bring The Final Call Newspaper to the door of every lost-found in the city and suburbs. He maps out the territory based on population density and location and lays out block by block the task of bringing the truth of our newspaper to the people.

He presses on the minds of the Believers that the sale of the paper is walking in the footsteps of the prophets. He teaches the men how to overcome "no." He teaches them how to properly deal with rejection and how to soldier forth under all circumstances. He eliminates the "I don't have time" excuse and all other excuses for not selling the paper. He continually teaches the history of Muhammad Speaks and what that generation of believers accomplished. He teaches on how this is the duty of every F.O.I and how this is part of our training in becoming Saviours of our people. He teaches the men of the reward that they will earn for themselves and their families by spreading the word.

The propagation officer reports on the progress of each Believer toward reaching the goal of 100 customers. He works with those whose progress has stalled. He ensures that the Believers are never alone in the field and always work in teams or with partners. He ensures the safety of the men while they are in the field and is always aware of field activity that is taking place.

PRODUCT

The product of this post is the steady and sustained increase of the circulation of The Final Call Newspaper delivered to the homes of the lost-found. These customers will form the base for all other products and services that we will, in time, offer. We will raise the sales in Chicago significantly enough to ensure that the National Center is economically independent of all other mosques.

Qualifications

The Propagation Officer, above all else, has to lead by example. He must be clearly on the path to 100 customers. He has to be zealous in his desire to get the Truth to our people. He has to be inspiration to the Believers. He must be able to keep the Believers working cheerfully. He should have a thorough knowledge of the metropolitan area. He should be able to recite the answers to Lesson Number 1 of the Supreme Wisdom. **He should have a stable domestic life.**

1		Propagation Officer SOP manual	In development
2		The Proper Way of Handling People	Available
3		How to Master the Art of Sales	Available
4		Statistics of the Black Population in the area	Available

Check List of Tools Required for Post of Propagation Officer

If the student minister and the student captain forget or do not have time to keep the enthusiasm of The Final Call Newspaper operation up, the Propagation Officer must be allowed to do so.

From here, the mindset can really be allowed to Nation Build. Now we can pool our resources with like-minded individuals for group operations that allow us to quickly do as we are taught by the Honorable Minister Louis Farrakhan, which is to steal away. There has been no other time in history so serious where the words "do for self" directly relate to our survival, our independence, our freedom, our justice and our equality.

All praise is due to Allah for the coming of Master Fard Muhammad, the Great Mahdi for **reproducing** himself in the Most Honorable Elijah Muhammad, the Master teacher. All praise is due to Allah for the Most Honorable Elijah Muhammad's **reproduction** of himself into the Honorable Minister Louis Farrakhan. And all praise is due to Allah for the Honorable Minister Louis Farrakhan's divine wisdom and vision in guiding us.

This writing is purely inspired by the Honorable Minister Louis Farrakhan. There would be no Final Call if it were not for the Minister and the two that back him.

And for those of us that can "close the gap" and remain obedient, we too will be **reproduced** into the gods we were born to be. For this is our way of devotion. #ThePATH

****

Brother Chad "Ocho Cinco" Johnson

Recap

So now let's recap:

- Know what The Final Call newspaper is and what it consists of.
- Find a personal motivation for representing The Final Call newspaper.
- You MUST know the seeds of the P.A.T.H.
- Know that FEAR is an illusion.

- Consistently practice prayer and visualization techniques.
- Conquer the illusion of fear.
- Carry out the action.
- Be an example for the new Fruit.
- Include your wife into your mission, so she can be your peace.
- Take care of your health and your feet

In This Order

Start your day with prayer and meditation. Set your goals. Go over your to do list. You must fully hydrate yourself with alkaline water before you even leave your home. Look in the mirror. Are you well groomed? If there are nose hairs coming out of your nose, trim them. Make sure you shower each morning and evening.

Taking into consideration you are dressed to impress and you're wearing a great fragrance and look pleasing to the eye, I now need you to visualize with me. Imagine yourself walking up to the driver's side of a vehicle with an extended handshake or see yourself walking up to a residence or business. As the person opens the door or the person rolls down their window to shake your hand, you simultaneously say, "How are you?" or "How are you feeling today, King/ Queen? How are you doing today sir/ma'am?"

Listen carefully to their response. Acknowledge their response, and then ease this statement into your response: "We are in the neighborhood attempting to make our community a decent and safer place to live."

Now lift up The Final Call with your left hand and point to the $2 on the front of The Final Call with your right index finger and say: "If $2 is too much, we are grateful for whatever God puts on your heart" or "We are asking if you would be willing to make a $24 donation to help us in our cause in doing so. This includes a 10 week subscription to make sure that your smile is visible and wait for the many blessings that await you." Whether the person supports your cause or not, genuinely thank them for their time and move on to the next vehicle, business or home. Don't forget to offer a business card and mosque flyer. Remember, you are planting seeds, and you don't see the flower the same day you plant the seed.

Here's a scenario that I encounter every time I'm out in the field, especially on door-to-door campaigns. After I greet the person:

Me: We are now here in this community attempting to do our part in making the community a decent and safer place to live.

Them: Well, what is it that you will be doing in the neighborhood?

Me: We are taught that the basis of community development is self-improvement. So first we deal with the basics of knowledge of self, self-discipline, health etc. Then from there we take ourselves as examples into the community for others to see and bear witness to these examples.

Them: What do you do?

You: (You can either name what you have done in your city, or you can name things that we've accomplished in the Nation of Islam. After all, we are one. I like to name events that are national and international etc.) The Million Man March, trash pick-ups, health seminars, our men/women classes, crisis intervention with drug and gang violence, everything that we have done and are doing on a political, national, and local level. You can talk about all of the books the Most Honorable Elijah Muhammad and the Honorable Minister Louis Farrakhan have written and the purpose of each book. I can go on and on.

Them: Well, what do you believe in?

You: (You can inform them that they can read the back page) or you can explain: We believe in the one God who created the heavens and the earth and everything in between; and all the prophets that he sent.

Them: Who is that one God?

You: (At this point, General order #9 must be implemented for the sake of reaching more people. You ask them if you can come back to discuss these issues at a later date since you have a goal or quota to meet, this could take some time. Hand them a flyer and ask them if they would like to donate to help develop the community.) I often let our people know that regardless of what we believe as individuals, community development has proven to be more effective when we work together. "After all God is one." Once again, "May God continue to bless you and everyone in this household with a peaceful day." Then I move on. I don't waste time with debates unless I have the time, and I'm fully prepared.

Divine Reminder: ***"But I have this against you, that you have left your first love. Remember therefore from where you have fallen, and repent and do the deeds you did at first; or else I'm coming to you, and will remove your lampstand out of its place – unless you repent."*** (Revelations, Chapter 2: 4-5)

"Those who propagate the faith through delivering The Final Call Newspaper may not see themselves...but I see you and the Honorable Minister Louis Farrakhan sees you as a very intricate part of our nation.

One of the greatest tools to deliver the truth to our people is the Final Call Newspaper. Every time you look at a Black man you are looking at God. He who is a great propagator of the faith is a great servant of Allah. Look at the greatest post that we have. Our life is the greatest post that we have. Know that we are to walk our post in a perfect manner, keeping always on the alert.

We have accepted the post of Propagator of the Faith. Wiping away our sins depends on how we walk our post in a perfect manner and how we propagate the faith. We all have sinned and fall short of the glory of God. The problem is that we quit our post before we are properly relieved.

The Honorable Minister Louis Farrakhan is teaching us that it is a treasonous act if we quit our post before we are properly relieved. If we stop serving the people life through the word of Allah, this could mean our life also.

On behalf of the Supreme Captain and the laboring staff here at Mosque Maryam, we thank you and we appreciate all that you do in the way of propagating the faith. We are fighting for Islam and we will SURELY win."

Assistant Supreme Captain Grandmaster Anthony Muhammad

These are my Top 10 One-Liners (Add them to your own):

1) How are you doing? We are trying to help reduce violence in our community, and we think it's going to take more than marching and protesting. What do you think?

2) $2 donation to your own Black Nation.

3) $2 donation to help us do what we have to do in order to make our community a decent and safer place to live.

4) Any kind of donation to help us do what we have to do in our own community...I'll even turn in those coins you have in your ashtray.

5) 8 quarters, 20 dimes, 40 nickels...I'll even turn in 200 pennies if that's all you have.

6) All that money we spend with Koreans, Arabs, and other nationalities God isn't good for a $2?

7) We waste money every day on cookies and chips, we are just trying to save a life or change a life for the better.

8) It's going to take more than marching and protesting to save our people. It's going to take more than religion.

9) We are the same organization that brought you the Million Man March; we are the same organization that produced Muhammad Ali, Malcolm X and the Honorable Minister Louis Farrakhan.

10) The Final Call is a message dedicated to the Black man and woman of America and the world.

My Way of Giving Back To My Nation by The Late and Great Brother Khalil Muhammad

Elite 50 Final Call Newspaper Pioneer

Under the leadership of the Honorable Elijah Muhammad, Brother Khalil began soldiering in 1965. At that time, the newspaper was called Muhammad Speaks. Along with the newspaper, Brother Khalil made a nice living selling whiting fish. Following the instructions of the Honorable Minister Louis Farrakhan, He sold papers hand-to-hand in Chicago up into the year 2005, averaging 1300 Final Call Newspapers per issue. Brother Khalil started with one bundle (100 Newspapers) an issue. Each week, he would go up sometimes two and three bundles an issue.

For several weeks, Brother Khalil would average 1200 Final Call Newspapers an issue until he topped out at 2300 per issue. One of the things that amazed me was that he was in his mid 70's distributing the paper on 79th and Stony Island in Chicago. And it was on 79th and Stony Island in Chicago where I would study Brother Khalil and later follow in his footstep. I studied his dedication. I studied his consistency. But most of all, I studied how warm and receptive the people were to him.

The people loved him, the people respected him. The people were so loyal to Brother Khalil, that even though I was his protégé', they would not purchase The Final Call Newspaper from me unless he let them know that it was okay. And until he was 89 years of age, he pushed The Final Call Newspaper along with bean pies and the books, CD's and DVD's of both the Most Honorable Elijah Muhammad and the Honorable Minister Louis Farrakhan. Our brother departed the following year at 90 years old.

I remember interviewing Brother Khalil several years ago and I asked him what his motivation was? And in that meek, humble voice that many of us can still hear, he responded, "This was my way of giving back to my Nation."

As his protégé, I couldn't have said it any better.

LONG LIVE MUHAMMAD

Photo by Justin "Jmillz" Milhouse

Citations:

Copyright 2012, **The P.A.T.H.** Volume One by Hashim Hakim

The Holy Quran, Maulana Muhammad Ali, New 2002 Edition.

Copyright **Closing the Gap** by Jabril Muhammad,

The P.A.T.H. Volume One: A guidebook for soldiers involved in the resurrection work

BY ASHAHED M. MUHAMMAD -ASSISTANT EDITOR- | LAST UPDATED: MAY 9, 2014 - 5:28:45 PM

"The Final Call is a wonderful newspaper, filled with knowledge and wisdom. Every newspaper is really a small book; so when you take The Final Call, and study it, and then deliver it to our people, you are doing the work of a minister." ***—The Honorable Minister Louis Farrakhan***

***

Behind this book is an idea.

The idea is that one can share personal experiences to publicly reveal past insecurities and failures without fear of being judged, and then—via the written word—communicate those experiences to others that they may benefit.

It sounds simple, doesn't it? But it isn't. We live in a society where individuals are hesitant to share their mistakes and failures with others for fear of showing weakness. This is a very competitive society in which one who reaches a level of success in any field of endeavor often chooses to keep their effective strategies a secret for fear of empowering others who could one day challenge them for dominance, position or power.

"The P.A.T.H." by Hashim Hakim delivers techniques for hand-to-hand and door-to-door distribution of *The Final Call* Newspaper. This is important. *The Final Call* is an iconic and beloved institution within Black communities across the globe, and whether you know it or not, many Black people take pride in knowing that there is one authentic, uncompromised voice of truth available to the people. There is information and news analysis contained within those pages you will not find in any other publication.

"The P.A.T.H." (Patience Attraction Technique Humility) won't take very long to read. It is described as a workbook and manual. When you hear the word "manual", you might think of an owner's guide or a user's guide for an object. This is more like a guidebook that can be used to assist one in a specific field, but the terms manual and workbook are appropriate. There are quizzes at the end of the chapters, as well as areas to take notes. Great idea to encourage interaction with the materials.

Hashim's book not only delivers very real and practical suggestions on "how-to" distribute *The Final Call*, but even more importantly, it explains WHY one should become involved in that effort by doing their part to spread the truth and inform others. Once the WHY is explained then the HOW is much easier to accomplish. Why is that? Because once the WHY is known, desire grows, and since desire feeds the will, this acts as fuel to motivate you to remove anything within your sphere acting as a barrier preventing you from accomplishing your goals, whether it is in the area of *Final Call* distribution, or other areas of your spiritual journey. Hashim does an excellent job of using himself as an example demonstrating how his personal journey can be instructive for others coming into the mission. He speaks of his trials and tribulations, but he does not overdo it, and does not share them in a cheap attempt to gain sympathy. What he shares is his attempt to connect with the reader in a sincere and heartfelt way to show that he is a Black man, a Muslim, and a brother in the Nation of Islam just like many others striving daily, working towards self-improvement while at the same time battling all of the internal and external factors and temptations threatening to take us all off the straight path.

He shares with readers his initial fear of approaching people he didn't know to sell them *The Final Call* newspaper, which I found to be remarkable and unbelievable. Watching him work today, you would never have thought that. What Hashim Hakim has demonstrated is his ability to maintain the right spirit, the proper motivation, and steadfast consistency to become a legendary *Final Call* newspaper distributor. Moreover, his desire to teach and train others with the goal of creating an army of highly competent distributors like him nationwide to assist the Honorable Minister Louis Farrakhan by effectively distributing the truth contained in *The Final Call* throughout America and the world is worthy of praise.

And his methods appear to be working.

A quick glance at Hashim's Facebook page shows testimonials from young men who have gone up, not only in the quantity of paper sales, but they have described an increase in their levels of confidence and spirit as well.

Although it is the primary theme, Hashim's guidance contained in the book is not limited to the sale of *The Final Call*. Included are historical anecdotes regarding the Muhammad Speaks newspaper and *The Final Call* that some may not know. He also includes valuable fishing techniques that will aid in bringing visitors to the mosque. In addition, he places great emphasis on prayer and visualization as an important foundational portion of the resurrection work.

After finishing "The P.A.T.H." you may not become the top *Final Call* distributor in your city overnight—but then again, you just might!

(Hashim Hakim's book is currently available through Amazon, Kindle, IBooks, and many more outlets.

Contact for booking / Hashim Hakim

Phone Number: 904-426-2397

Email: thepathmethod@gmail.com or hashimmcjw@gmail.com

InstaGram: @thepath01

Facebook: On the P.A.T. H. (Group)

Testimonials:

Arthur 3X, Mecca (Detroit)

Having taken several personal observational NOTES from Hashim, it has really broadened my approach to the actual engagement of the people. There is a fine line between engaging and being confrontational in getting after our people, and I believe that's where the success is. Well that, and really having a heart for THE MISSION.

Warren Muhammad, Atlanta

I first experienced The P.A.T.H. in action with Bro Hashim in Orlando, Florida when I was part of the Orlando Study Group. The most important part that stuck with me is the introduction. To be specific, shaking the hands of the customer and asking them, "how are you doing?" That may seem insignificant, however, to me, it is the most important part because it breaks down any possible defense the customer may have and shows an interest in their well-being. After that, to close the deal is easy. So I have incorporated The P.A.T.H. in my distribution of The Final Call and in Atlanta, I was awarded the pin for being a bundle brother two years ago.

Student Regional Captain Stephen Muhammad, Southwest Region

In the name of Allah the Beneficent, the most Merciful God! I bear witness that there is no god but He and that Muhammad is indeed His Messenger!
We are soldiers that have accepted the responsibility of shouldering The Mission of the Resurrection given to the Most Honorable Elijah Muhammad and his principal helper, the Honorable Minister Louis Farrakhan by God Himself! The P.A.T.H. has absolutely put me on the path of mastering my "craft" which is the delivery of the word of God contained in that mighty fine independent Black-Owned newspaper called "The Final Call." Using the techniques and strategies that are presented in the P.A.T.H has improved my sales....I did say "sales"...hello somebody! And even though that is the case, that's not the motivation. But because of the proper motivation and technique, your sales will markedly improve! I use the P.A.T.H. everytime I'm out delivering the FCN and I'm always, always successful....I know how to get a "win" with every interaction, no matter if there was a sale or not. This will keep your spirit up and when you have the right spirit and right motivation along with the right technique, then we will by the grace of Almighty God Allah be successful! The Battle is ours but the victory belongs to Allah! I certainly use and recommended the P.A.T.H. to all of the mighty soldiers of Allah that have "accepted" The Mission of the Most Honorable Elijah Muhammad called The Resurrection of the dead!

Brother Walter, Gainesville/Jacksonville, FL

When Brother Hashim introduced me to The P.A.T.H, it helped me realize that I'm not just going out to sell papers, but I'm going out to deliver the truth to our people. He said that we must understand we are Saviours first, then salesmen.

Brother Jamell

With the grace of Allah, Brother Hashim has laid out an easy to follow blueprint when distributing The Final Call Newspaper. By using the four steps explained in The P.A.T.H., I've been able to distribute 100 Final Call Newspapers In 4-6 hours every Saturday since receiving my X. Allah U Akbar!

Made in the USA
Monee, IL
21 February 2023